Praise for

DOWN CITY

"Carroll proceeds from these haunting twin plot points [her parents' deaths] through a patchwork of vignettes, reportage and reflection that reaches after her absent parents with sensitive longing.... Carroll's writing is most evocative when she describes, with a heartbreaking mixture of tenderness and disappointment, the moments of intimate connection between her and her father."

—*New York Times Book Review*

"Carroll grasps fleeting moments and memories with confidence and disarming delicacy.... So rich in mood, feeling, and genuine love, this investigative memoir is a true tribute." —*Booklist* (starred review)

"An unusual, mesmerizing hybrid: part true-crime story, part coming-of-age memoir, part portrait of a parent's alcoholism, part love letter to Rhode Island." —*Vice*

"Carroll's understated prose complements this daunting material, and her struggles as an unhappy, rebellious teen seem almost idyllic in contrast to the dysfunction and tragedy that shadow her... Carroll's determined grappling with the burden of her past is honestly and skillfully done."

—*Publisher's Weekly* (Starred Review)

"Carroll's quietly powerful story offers a courageous, clear-eyed vision of a broken family while exploring the meaning of forgiveness. An honest and probing memoir of coming to terms with family."

—*Kirkus*

" It's an emotional, high stakes ride as Leah discovers her mother's love for life, talent for photography, and the drug addiction that ultimately let to her murder. Leah's prose is beautiful, rich and dark. With each turn of the page you find yourself laughing…then feeling truly broken for Leah….Leaves the reader nostalgic and in awe."

—*Providence Monthly*

"Harrowing and deeply personal, this memoir about the author's alcoholic manic-depressive father and mother who was brutally murdered by drug dealers will keep you engaged until the very last page."

—*InStyle*

"Tough and dreamy, searching and sad, this debut memoir by a collateral victim of murder delves deep."

—*Library Journal*

"Honest, unsettling and inspiring…it proves the resiliency of human nature and uncovers the talent of a gifted writer."

—*Winnipeg Free Press*

"Affecting.... Heartbreaking as it is, Carroll's book is equally enthralling."

—Bustle.com

"Leah Carroll's DOWN CITY drops us into a family story heavy with secrets and crackling with regret. Hers is a portrait of two parents straining desperately to find their better angels, and a daughter whose resilience is tested again and again. The fact that she proves herself both survivor and frank and generous curator of their story is a great gift, both to their memory and to readers alike."

—Megan Abbott, bestselling author of
The Fever and *You Will Know Me*

"Leah Carroll's writing is vivid and honest, and DOWN CITY is a clear-eyed act of regaining a father by artfully cataloging his loss."

—Charles Graeber, *New York Times*
bestselling author of *The Good Nurse:
A True Story of Medicine, Madness, and Murder*

"Quick and clear as glass, evocative and engaging, DOWN CITY is a story of a daughter's moving search for the truth about the parents whose dark complexities have left a mystery at the center of her existence."

—George Hodgman, author of *Bettyville*

"Leah Carroll's Rhode Island is seedy, charismatic, broke-down, and irresistible: so much like the characters in her gripping heartbreak of a memoir. Only a writer as brave in her heart as she is on the page could make us love the ghosts she chases through police reports, memory, and the desolate landmarks of her own tragedy. Leah Carroll is that writer, proving that no matter who haunts you or for how long, only forgiveness can set you free."

—Melissa Febos, author of
Whip Smart and *Abandon Me*

"Driven by a ferocious demand for justice, Leah Carroll takes us with her as she extricates herself from layer after layer of lies, determined not only to find but to understand the truth about her parents' tragic lives. DOWN CITY is a riveting and heartbreaking inquiry, born of inner necessity, and written in a deceptively simple and deeply affecting prose that elevates its storytelling to art."

—Richard Hoffman, author of
Half the House and *Love & Fury*

DOWN CITY

A Daughter's Story of Love, Memory, and Murder

Leah Carroll

GRAND CENTRAL
PUBLISHING

NEW YORK   BOSTON

Copyright © 2017 by Leah Carroll
Jacket design by Lisa Honerkamp
Jacket photograph by Joan Goldman Carroll
Cover copyright © 2017 by Hachette Book Group, Inc.

Grand Central Publishing
Hachette Book Group
1290 Avenue of the Americas, New York, NY 10104
grandcentralpublishing.com
twitter.com/grandcentralpub

First published in hardcover and ebook in March 2017.
First Trade Paperback Edition: March 2018.

Grand Central Publishing is a division of Hachette Book Group, Inc. The Grand Central Publishing name and logo is a trademark of Hachette Book Group, Inc.

The publisher is not responsible for websites (or their content) that are not owned by the publisher.

The Hachette Speakers Bureau provides a wide range of authors for speaking events. To find out more, go to www.hachettespeakersbureau.com or call (866) 376-6591.

Photographs by Joan Goldman Carroll

Library of Congress Cataloging-in-Publication Data

Names: Carroll, Leah, author.
Title: Down city : a daughter's story of love, memory, and murder / Leah Carroll.
Description: First Edition. | New York : Grand Central Publishing, 2017.
Identifiers: LCCN 2016029300| ISBN 9781455563319 (hardback) | ISBN 9781478904847 (audio download) | ISBN 9781455563302 (e-book)
Subjects: LCSH: Carroll, Leah. | Murder—Rhode Island. | Drug abuse and crime—Rhode Island. | BISAC: BIOGRAPHY & AUTOBIOGRAPHY / Women.
Classification: LCC HV6533.R4 C37 2017 | DDC 361.452/3092—dc23 LC record available at https://lccn.loc.gov/2016029300

ISBN: 978-1-4555-6329-6 (trade paperback)

Printed in the United States of America

LSC-C

10 9 8 7 6 5 4 3 2 1

FOR RUTH AND LOUIS GOLDMAN

DOWN CITY

PART ONE

PROLOGUE

———— •=•— ————

On the night she died, my mom drove to a motel to buy cocaine with two men: Peter Gilbert and Gerald Mastracchio. Once inside, Gilbert watched television while Mastracchio spread the cocaine on a table and demanded sex from my mother. She complied. Years later, Gilbert would testify that "Mastracchio emerged from the bathroom with a towel, threw it around Carroll's neck and yanked. Mastracchio grunted to Gilbert for help as Carroll's face turned purple. 'Come on you rat,' Mastracchio wheezed. 'Give me the death rattle.'"

This happened at the Sunset View Motel in Attleboro, Massachusetts, just minutes from the Rhode Island border. It was October 18, 1984. My mother was thirty. Her name was Joan Carroll. I had just turned four years old.

AT THE SPORTSMAN'S Inn, rooms rented for forty dollars a week. The ground floor was a strip club with a 24-hour Italian buffet. This is where Kevin Carroll, my father, died on December 28, 1998. That morning, the proprietor of the Sportsman's Inn tried to open the door to my father's room. He couldn't. My father's dead body was blocking it. He was forty-eight years old. I was eighteen.

Later, the funeral director gave me his possessions in a plastic bag: a Montblanc pen, an expired identification card from his job at the *Providence Journal*, roughly two hundred dollars in cash and change, and a pair of reading glasses.

WHO WERE THESE people, my parents, and how did they come to this place?

ONE

———— •❖• ————

One of my first memories: I'm eating a TV dinner. Each part of the meal is in its own little tinfoil compartment. I love the bright-green peas, the square of crusty, salted mashed potatoes, and the rectangle of Salisbury steak. I eat in front of the TV, my legs folded under a tray.

I'm talking to my dad but I call him Kevin, which is his name.

"Kevin, Kevin, Kevin, Daddy's name is Kevin."

Suddenly, my dad is out of his chair. He grabs me under the shoulders, knocking over the tray. Salisbury steak splatters on the wooden floor, peas roll in all directions. Dad pushes my bedroom door open with his foot, lets go of my armpits with a push, and I'm sailing through the air. I land on my bed, too stunned at first to cry. I bob up and down on my waterbed, dumbstruck. Finally, I let out a long wail. My leg hurts from where it hit the wooden bed frame and I cry, curling into a ball in the middle of the big undulating bed. Later, Mom comes into the room and pulls me onto her lap. She wipes at my grimy face with her hands.

"Leah, Leah," she says, stroking my head, "what are we going to do with you?"

"You're not going to call the police, are you?"

She looks at me for a few seconds and then runs her fingers through my hair. "No, sweetie," she says. "We would never call the police."

✦

MOM AND DAD teach me all the words to "Rock 'N' Roll High School" by the Ramones, and Mom and I make up a dance to Michael Jackson's "Beat It." I use the coffee table as my stage and Mom and Dad blast the music on the record player and I know all the words and we dance around the living room, the dogs jumping and barking and going crazy around our feet.

At night I wake up and Dad is screaming at Mom. I walk into the living room where Mom sits on the couch and Dad stands by the window. Mom's yellow mutt, Brandy, is curled at her feet, and his tail thumps against the ground when I come in. Dad's boxer, Ali, sits next to him, ears alert.

Dad says, "We're fighting because I want your mom to quit smoking."

He crosses his arms over his PAWTUCKET PIRATES softball T-shirt, the one with the skull.

I sit on the couch next to Mom and Brandy puts his head between us. Sometimes when he goes to the bathroom his poop is orange, and Mom says it's because he has cancer. I love him so much that sometimes I squeeze him extra hard, trying to hurt him just a little bit, and he lets me. He's a ragged-looking dog, missing patches of yellow hair. Dad's dog, Ali, wins prizes at dog shows and follows Dad around adoringly. When my mom takes photos they pose with the same proud expression and upturned face. But Ali is too strong for me and once he chewed my kitchen play set to bits.

"You shouldn't smoke, Mom," I say. "It's bad for you."

Mom cries again, which makes Brandy skittish. He staggers on his weak hind legs and backs up a few paces. I don't want Mom to smoke and get cancer like Brandy.

———✦———

DURING THE DAY Mom unfurls long strips of film to dry on a string over the bathtub and sometimes she lets me stand in the tiny closet next to the bathroom where she flips on a red lightbulb and warns me not to touch any of the chemicals. We watch the paper go from white to gray and then shapes begin to form as she swirls the paper around with a pair of tongs. Images of Ali and Dad appear like magic.

Most of the time my mom and I are a secret team, keeping secrets from my dad. She tells me we're going to take the city bus because her car is getting fixed and this sounds like a great adventure. We take the bus to her friend's house in Providence and she leaves me there in the living room, where I watch television until the room begins to darken. I sit on the floor pulling at long strands of orange carpet, wondering what is up the stairs. There are no stairs at our house.

When she comes back we get on the bus again. Mom says, "Isn't this fun?" and I nod, because it is kind of fun, the way the bus lurches and wheezes around the city. "If you want to do this again you can't tell Dad where we were. If you tell Dad I'll get in big trouble and we won't be able to ride the bus again. Do you understand?" She kisses the top of my head.

Later, Mom drives me in Grandma's car to a small house with long steps leading up to the front door from the street. She takes the keys from the ignition and tells me to wait in the car. She leans over and pats the space beneath the dashboard, telling me to get down there and stay until she comes back. "I'll lock the doors," she says.

After a few seconds, I peek out the car window and watch her go up the stairs to the house. She wears a black leather jacket, tight at the hips. She walks up, up all those stairs. And then she's out of sight.

———•———

I AM FOUR years old and we're going to Grandma and Grandpa's house. Mom has packed my stuff into a blue

American Tourister suitcase. Her car smells like cigarettes but also something sweet. It's my favorite smell. I snap the brass buckles on the suitcase open and closed.

"I don't want to go to Grandma's house, again," I say. Mom is silent in the front seat.

When we get there, Mom takes my suitcase into the house. Grandma wipes the counter in the kitchen with a damp towel. I hug her around the knees and say, "I love you, Grandma, but I don't want to stay over anymore."

Grandma smiles like she doesn't hear and kisses my cheek. She looks like my mom, but with white hair. The inside of her pocketbook smells like lipstick and sugarless gum. I like to sneak it open and leave her love notes and drawings. I steal tissues from the little package she keeps inside and look at myself in her compact mirror. I put on her sunglasses and pretend to be her, hands around the imaginary steering wheel of her big blue Dodge, purse strap hanging off my shoulder.

Grandpa sits, where he always sits, in his reclining chair in the den. His dog, Spot, snores on his lap. Spot only gets up from the chair when Grandpa gets up. Spot's name is funny because his fur is all black. No spots.

Grandpa tells a lot of jokes I don't get and sings old-fashioned songs like, *Hey good lookin' / what you got cookin'?* Sometimes we watch *The Three Stooges* and Grandpa laughs and laughs. He tells me that the Stooges were Jewish, just like us.

I start crying so Grandpa will notice me. I tell him, "Mom says we have to stay over again."

Grandpa doesn't look away from the TV screen. "Knock, knock," he says.

I sniff wetly and keep my head buried in my knees. "Who's there?"

"Boo."

"Boo who?" I ask.

"Whaddya cryin' for?" He looks at me, waiting for my laugh. I wipe my face on the crocheted afghan and Grandpa adjusts the TV antenna with his foot.

Mom kisses Grandpa on the forehead and says, "Leah, if you don't stop crying, you won't get your present."

I run after her into the kitchen where a big cardboard box waits for me. On the front is a picture of a vacuum, a broom, and a mop. Grandma gets scissors from a drawer and says, "Here, Lee-lee, I'll do it."

Together we pull out the miniature cleaning supplies. I stroke the ropy ends of the mop imagining all the games I will play with these toys. I can be a mom, cleaning the house and yelling at the kids. I can be an orphan who has to clean the whole house before the orphanage lady comes back and beats me. I can be a princess, locked away by an evil witch and made to clean my dungeon. I barely notice as Mom kisses me and walks out the door. I hear her car rev up and out of the driveway as I push my broom around the orange-and-brown linoleum. Grandma ties a bandanna around my head so I can be just like a real maid.

———•———

AT NIGHT, GRANDMA lets me wear one of her velour housecoats over my pajamas. It goes down past my feet and as we walk down the stairs Grandma holds up the back and says, "Careful, careful," with each step. We make our special nighttime snack by pouring peanuts and big fat golden raisins into a bowl and then shaking them until they are all mixed together. Grandma lets me have a spoonful of peanut butter, and I lick the spoon as we walk into the den and sit on the couch.

"That kid's nuts for peanuts," Grandpa says, and he and Grandma laugh. Grandma thinks all of Grandpa's jokes are funny.

I wake to Grandma lifting me off the sofa. Grandpa snores in his chair. I fell asleep halfway through *Murder, She Wrote*, which is kind of scary but mostly not, because Jessica Fletcher is an old lady.

I wonder when we are going home to the little house on Dixwell Avenue. We stay with Grandma and Grandpa for what feels like a long, long time.

———•———

ONE MORNING I wake up and the sun shines bright through the window beside me, but where Mom should be, the bed is untouched. I walk down the stairs and into the kitchen where Aunty Sandy and Grandma are standing by the counter.

"Mom's not home," I say.

Grandma bends over the kitchen table and starts to cry. She and Aunty Sandy talk about Mom's car. Aunty Sandy says she wants to go out and look for it again. Grandma says we should call and let the police do that. Grandpa is in the den, sitting in the recliner, watching TV.

"Where's Mom?" I ask again.

Grandma goes to the den to tell Grandpa they are leaving. He turns briefly from the television to look at her. "We'll be right back," she says to me. Her face is splotchy from crying and her lipstick is worn away from her mouth. Her breath smells like coffee.

When they leave I halfheartedly mop the floor with my toy mop, but it isn't as fun without a bandanna tied around my head, and Grandma is the one who does that for me. I go to the living room, with its china closets and sofa I'm not allowed to sit on. There are pictures in beautiful silver frames set up on a table in front of the bay window. I make the faces in the frames talk to each other.

"Hi, Kevin and Joan," I make a picture of my Aunty Sandy say to a picture of my parents. In the picture my aunt looks extra pretty. She wears a green shirt that says ARMY and big silver earrings.

"Hi, Leah," I make a picture of my mom say to me. "Here I am," says the picture. "Here I am. Here I am. Here I am."

FOR MONTHS AFTER my mom disappears, my grandmother and I live in a world of make-believe. It's like Mister

Rogers' Neighborhood of Make-Believe, but there is no King Friday or Queen Saturday. There is no shy Daniel Striped Tiger. Mister Rogers never pops up at the beginning of our day to narrate what happened the day before.

He never says, "Yesterday in Grandma and Leah's world of make-believe they went to the Rhode Island Mall. And Leah asked Grandma if they could sit in the pit in the middle filled with fake trees where all the old men smoke cigarettes, and Grandma said, 'No, of course not,' and that Leah 'should never smoke because smoking kills you.' And Leah thought, *But Mom smokes.*"

The difference between our world of make-believe and the regular world is that in our world of make-believe my mom is still alive. In the real world, my mom's body will remain off the side of the highway, undiscovered for five months. But because there is no trolley car to signal the beginning and end of the make-believe, my grandma and I keep at it relentlessly.

———◆———

AT NIGHT I sleep in bed with Grandma. Grandpa, like always, sleeps in his recliner. Before we go to bed, Grandma and I say a Jewish prayer for protection. We open the small blue prayer book and read, "Oh Lord, grant that this night we may sleep in peace. And that in the morning our awakening may also be in peace. May our daytime be cloaked in your peace. Protect us and inspire us to think and act only out of love. Keep far from us all evil; may our paths be free from all obstacles from when we go out until we return home."

Then Grandma says, "Close the light," and I jump out of bed and flick the switch. "Now we pray for Joanie," she says as I climb back under the sheets. Grandma's head is covered in plastic rollers, and her nightdress makes a zipping sound as it rubs against the sheets. Her partial dentures sit in a glass of water on the nightstand. The pink and silver of them in the cobalt-tinted drinking glass look like jewelry to me, or treasure sunk to the bottom of the ocean.

"Dear God," says Grandma, "please bring Joanie home safe to us because we love her and miss her." Even then, as we pray, my mom seems to exist only in the world my grandma and I have created. Nobody else talks about her.

———•———

SOME MORNINGS, GRANDMA takes me to work with her at Klitzner Industries, a brick factory building in Providence producing pins and medals and emblems, and—the best thing—American flags inlaid with shiny red, white, and blue gemstones.

"Rhode Island," Grandma tells me, "is the costume jewelry capital of the world."

She pins a shining American flag on my jean jacket. I work on the adding machine, sending out a roll of narrow white paper covered in my own imaginary algebra. I calculate my age, Grandma's age, Mom's age, Brandy's age, Dad's age. I add them all together, then subtract them.

After work, we run errands. Sometimes when Mom had errands to do, she let me stay in the car, but Grandma is nervous about kidnappers, so she makes me go inside every place we stop. At the market, I pluck a grape as I roll past in the shopping cart. Grandma grabs it out of my hand.

"That's stealing," she says. Grandma never gets mad at me, just a little more nervous than usual, which is pretty nervous. She clutches the grape in her fist and looks around. "You could get arrested," she says.

I say, "Mom lets me eat grapes when we go shopping."

She looks at the waxy green grape in her hand and drops it into a bin of oranges.

———— ✦ ————

I think that things might stay like this forever—that it will be just me and Grandma and Grandpa—but then things change. The police find my mother's body and in March 1985 there is a funeral. Nobody tells me about it and I don't go. It's a secret but I'm the only one who doesn't know. Even though I kind of know.

TWO

————◆————

When she was alive, my mom drove a blue Volkswagen Scirocco. There was rust around the wheel wells, and inside it smelled like marzipan and cigarette smoke. I remember that car. I remember standing outside that car while my mom chatted with neighbors. I remember being lifted from the backseat of that car by a man in a uniform one rainy night when we drove through a puddle and the engine stalled. Was he a policeman? A tow truck driver? I don't remember that.

On the night my mom disappeared, October 18, 1984, she attended a Simchat Torah celebration with my grandmother at Temple Sinai, and then said she was going to meet a friend named Debbie. She promised to be back before eleven, and she reversed her sweet-smelling Scirocco out of the driveway at 65 Midland Drive, turned down the cul-de-sac, and was gone.

At nine thirty the next morning, she was still gone and my grandmother called the Cranston police. Officer Derrico drove to 65 Midland Drive and wrote the facts in his police report: We'd been living with my grandparents for the last month because my parents had separated. Last winter, my mother went to Edgehill for drug rehabilitation, but my grandmother was positive she'd since been behaving herself to the fullest.

Her daughter Joan would not, according to my grandmother, stay out all night without calling. She did not have any boyfriends. And she wouldn't leave her baby daughter without contacting my grandmother to tell her where she was. My grandmother could give a description of her car: a turquoise Volkswagen Scirocco, but she could not recall the plates. They were Rhode Island plates. Maybe they were KC-??? Or maybe they were PB-??? She tried, and had been trying, unsuccessfully to contact my father.

The officer patrolled the streets of Cranston from Knightsville to Meshanticut but was unable to locate any vehicle matching my grandmother's description. He took down my mom's description: Joan B. Carroll...DOB 4-6-54...5'1" tall...100 lbs....short brown hair...scar over one eye...LSW maroon print dress and tan heels.

The next day my grandmother called back. Officer Palmer reported to her house. She'd made contact with Joan's estranged husband, my dad, Kevin Carroll. The vehicle was registered in his name with RI plates KC38.

A 1975 Volkswagen Scirocco, color blue. The officer put out a broadcast to all cars in regard to the plate. Officer Davies reported that he knew the car, he knew the female, he had, in fact, stopped this female in her car several nights before. She was known to frequent the Atwood Avenue area, in particular Sonny Russo's Restaurant at Atwood and Fortini Street. An officer was dispatched to the location but neither the vehicle nor the female could be located.

There was no more information to report at that time except this: "Attention: Investigators...Mrs. Goldman is quite concerned as to possibly what might have happened and fears the worse [sic] about her daughter."

———•———

THIRTY YEAR LATER I sit on the back porch of my grandmother's house with my mother's childhood best friend, Audrey. She was interested in the Goldmans from the moment they moved to 65 Midland Drive. It was the early 1960s. Kennedy was president. My mom's family was the only family on the street without a Christmas tree in the window.

"My world," Audrey says, "was very white. It was very normal. Everyone was the same. I was fascinated by your mother. No Christmas tree! Everybody talked about the Jews next door."

Audrey is reluctant to go inside my grandmother's house. She doesn't feel like she can talk freely inside.

So we sit on the back deck holding enormous iced coffees from Dunkin' Donuts. The plastic cups of Dunkin' Donuts coffee sit inside a Styrofoam one. It's called a hot cup and you get one whether you ask or not in Rhode Island. One nonbiodegradable material inside another. The Styrofoam keeps your iced coffee cold and drip-free. I tried once to explain the hot cup to someone, laughing at how provincial it seemed. "But does it work?" they asked.

"Yeah," I said. My instinct had been to dismiss it. But it does work, really well.

We hear the cars speed by on Phenix Avenue, to the Warwick Mall maybe, or to the beaches, where you need to steel yourself for a full-body plunge—inch by inch is the fool's way into this part of the Atlantic. The moment the cold salt water slaps your belly, grown men shriek and make for the shore. But here on the porch, sweat drips down the back of my neck in the summer heat and everything smells like baking asphalt.

"I want you to know," Audrey says, "your mother and I, no matter how she died, no matter any of that, we were just giggly girls. We had the same sarcastic sense of humor. In a way, we thought we were better than everyone else. We didn't care about painting our nails or shaving our legs."

Audrey has fared well. Her face is the same kind one I remember from when she babysat me as a young girl. Her dark-brown hair has turned silver and is cut to her chin. "I didn't get clean right after your mom died. I knew I should, but I couldn't."

The sound of cars in the distance. We sit silent. And then, "Your mom had the rare ability to be one hundred percent honest. I could tell her anything and just by listening, somehow she made it better. When she was gone, I lost that." Audrey's crying now, big tears that cling to her chin before they splatter onto her knees.

"She was, and I mean this, she was a real person. She was a rebel, a kindred spirit. She was... she was delightful. For years I thought about her every day. But I haven't thought of her in a long time." She looks guilty when she says this.

If I were a better person I would tell her not to feel guilty. I would tell her that I hadn't really thought about my mom in thirty years. Not as a real person anyway. I would tell her it took me thirty years, thirty selfish, callow years, to realize my mom had been a human being, a woman, a person on her own and not an extension that ended where I began.

If I were a better person I probably would have also told the teenage girl at Dunkin' Donuts that I didn't need that hot cup and right then I'd be holding a sweaty, melting iced coffee and the whole world would continue to spin. But I'm not. Instead, I'm jealous of Audrey. I'm jealous of this woman and the grief she feels because I don't know the Joan Goldman Carroll she's talking about: my mother.

———◆———

ON OCTOBER 20, 1984, according to the police report, they located my mother's car. It was parked in front of 17 Mill Street in Johnston, Rhode Island. The engine was cold. One neighbor told them she remembered the car had been there at least since Thursday afternoon. Another neighbor said he didn't recognize the vehicle, did not remember seeing it in the past, and had not seen anyone leaving or returning to it.

My mother's pocketbook was in the car. In the pocketbook was a license and a ten-dollar bill. Inside the car there was also a NJ Registration 374 MXU license plate, which came back as "nothing in file" from the New Jersey Registry. The little blue Scirocco was taken to the police garage awaiting BCI for fingerprint examination.

Once the police released it, nobody knew what to do with the car. My father and my aunt covered it in a tarp and parked it behind a friend's garage so I wouldn't recognize it.

———◆———

"I GOT THAT car, you know," Audrey tells me, sweating on the porch behind my grandmother's house. "The Volkswagen—your dad gave it to me. It smelled like almonds. Something to do with the engine or transmission or something." This memory makes her weep but I feel vindicated. I knew I remembered that smell.

In all likelihood it's the heater core that gave it that smell. A leaking heater core that spilled onto the floor of the passenger side where the scent would linger long after the problem itself was actually fixed.

———•———

IN THE MARCH 9, 1977, edition of the *Providence Journal's Evening Bulletin*, two stories appeared side by side. Separating them are two photographs of my mom, the newly appointed Warwick dog officer. She's wearing a surprisingly official-looking uniform: heavy jacket over a crisp white dress shirt, buttoned to the top and fastened with a neat black ribbon. It's topped off by a black-brimmed hat to which is fastened a large gold badge. I can't make out the insignia but the badge is huge, almost comically oversized, replete with eagle wings spread across the top.

In the bottom picture my mom stands, hands on hips, in front of a cage marked NUMBER 4. It looks as if she has been snapped in the middle of speaking—she's looking into the cage, her hands are on her hips, and she seems, more than anything, uncomfortable. In the upper photo, the hat and badge loom over her downturned face as she looks down at a puppy she's cradling against her chest. In that photo, it's as if she doesn't realize anyone else is there.

In 1977 my mom is not yet my mom. She's Joan Goldman, twenty-three, who has "taken a veterinary assistant's course at Rhode Island Junior College and has had more than two years' experience as a dog groomer and kennel supervisor. Before she became dog officer, she cared for research animals at Roger Williams General Hospital in Providence."

In March 1977 my mom is still a few months away from meeting my dad. She has a real job for the first time in her life and it's a hard one: She has had to explain to the police chief that the dogs' kennels need to be papered or their joints will ache, that they need higher-quality food and stainless-steel dog bowls. She has had to beg a man not to surrender his black puppy, only to discover once he has left that the puppy's hind leg is broken.

Her fifth day on the job she has had to deal with controversy when seven dogs were nearly taken to the Providence facility to be gassed in violation of a city ordinance that says animals must be held at the pound for fifteen days before they are killed. She has had a confrontation with the president of Concerned Citizens for Dogs, "the city's most strident pound critic," who was able to have the van full of dogs halted only after an anonymous member who "keeps an eye on the pound" notified her of the violation.

And, while it doesn't say it in the article, on top of all that, my mom has shown up at my grandparents' house with seven dogs in need of adoption and she will slowly, over the course of several weeks, cajole and persuade friends and strangers to take them in. My grandfather winds up with a black puppy with a broken back leg that he names Spot, which is a joke, they'll explain to me later, because he doesn't have any spots. The last to go is an older dog, a large mutt. He's suspicious and not particularly pretty with long legs and short fur. He's territorial and bares his fangs and is devoted, utterly and completely, to his new owner, Joan Carroll, the Warwick dog officer. She names him Brandy.

———•———

IF I FOLD my photocopy of this article in half it's almost like seeing photos of two different women. On the bottom is the woman in the uniform, slightly uncomfortable in front of the camera but faking it with her hands on her hips. On the top is the woman cradling the puppy—that's who I thought my mom was growing up.

My family rarely talked about my mom once she was gone. It was my grandmother who most often brought her up. My mother loved animals. She led the other kids in funeral processions for all the pets—the hamsters and turtles and fish—that died in the neighborhood. She would deliver a solemn eulogy and all the other kids listened, even though she was the youngest.

My mother smiled all the time. She was so happy and so friendly and everywhere she went the room lit up and people exclaimed, "Joanie!" This is why—my grandmother would explain to a sullen twelve-year-old me—*I* should smile more. I used to think my grandmother was foolish for her constant ingratiation, the way she smiled even at surly pharmacists and drivers with the misfortune of being stuck behind her. I realize now it's how she survived. It's how she survived my mother's death, and my grandfather's mental illness, and fifty years at the same job, smiling and clicking away at her adding machine. And even today when she walks into a room, pale and unsteady, her brain all but wrecked from Alzheimer's, it's true that everyone rushes to greet her. "Ruthie!" they say, delighted by her.

But most important, my grandmother told me, my mom was smart. She was so clever and she read books all the time. Once, my grandmother showed me a story my mom had written for school. It was about four pages long, handwritten, and it was about a man who murdered a child. When I got to the final page it was revealed the man was the child's father, and he was horribly deformed and he had passed that deformity on to his son. The last line read, "It was a case of euthanasia." And then beneath that was a picture of the grotesque man, rendered in green and brown colored pencil. I wished that one day I could be that talented. I asked my grandmother what *euthanasia* meant. She wasn't sure.

My mother inherited my grandmother's petite frame with tiny wrists and large breasts. Before I was born my grandmother had a breast reduction. "They took out four pounds of flesh from one side and six from the other," she once said. She explained that when you were large-breasted you had to dress to cover it up or it's all anyone would notice. They were a curse, really. She hoped I wouldn't get them too. I've waited my whole life for those breasts to show up, but my grandma got her wish. And still I find I take fashion cues from her—shirts buttoned to the top and accented with a big necklace, maybe a brooch at the throat. I remember watching her in the mirror, taking off one necklace and holding another up to her neck, matching the accent in her paisley blouse to the amber beads.

My mother, though, had no need for fashion. She was a tomboy. She kept her hair short, she wore pants and T-shirts and plain blouses. I've seen two photos of her in a dress— one is her wedding day, in a beautiful empire-waisted ivory gown. In the second she is heavily pregnant with me and it must be one of those last few sizzling days that sneak up on you in September, because she's wearing a waist- less maternity dress and has bare legs and it is also, coin- cidentally, the only photo I have seen where she looks utterly and completely miserable. It's the look of misery I've seen since on women in the last few weeks before they give birth, uncomfortable in any position, unable to sleep, everything swollen. It's a picture I love, because for years my mom was described to me as practically beatific, a tiny woman cradling a lost puppy, a smiling sprite dancing into a room. But in this photo there's no pretense. It's hot. She's huge. She's not in the mood to mug for the camera. She wants me out of her.

"Your mom was wild," my aunt tells me. She tells me

how at night my mom would dangle from the sill of the second-story bedroom the sisters shared and plop onto the grass below, my aunt's heart in her throat every time she did it. And then she was off.

"We were hippies," Audrey tells me. "We wanted to hitchhike to the beach and we wanted to hang out in old-man bars and we didn't want to do anything people expected us to."

In 1968, the same year my father was dropping out of high school in tenth grade and signing up to go to Vietnam, my mom was fourteen. Everyone around her was getting high. I found a stash of letters in my grandmother's closet once, the letters written in response to her letters to boys from her high school who'd gone off to war. They talked about the music they were listening to and what they'd do when they came home. They talked, more than once, about trying heroin, about how my mom should stay away from it.

My mom was also always a woman who took in strays. Stray dogs and stray people. The stories go that she one time clung to the side of a moving city bus, pounding on the door, after the driver refused to pick up a handicapped woman; that she was constantly on the lookout for injustice, volunteering to visit the patients at the Institute for Mental Health.

"We used to joke that we were social workers," Audrey tells me. "Everyone would come to us because they thought we had our shit together. We'd be at a party doing God knows what and people would be coming to your mom for advice and she'd try to help them and then she'd say to me, 'Audrey, I think I'm probably more fucked up than anyone else here, don't they notice?'"

As the story goes, she met my father at a party. I try to imagine it, my dad home from Vietnam, his mustache and long hair, high-end stereo equipment, and Rickenbacker bass guitar. The two of them, like celestial bodies, party-goers orbiting around them until, inevitably, the two most charismatic people in the room collide in an explosion of wit, and charm, and no sense whatsoever that they were not invincible. The only thing my mom couldn't believe was that a man as handsome as my dad would be attracted to a woman as plain as she believed herself to be. The cute one. The tomboy.

———•———

MY FATHER RARELY talked about my mom. I know now they were separated when she died, that they likely would have gotten a divorce. But there was something wistful in the way he talked about her on the rare occasions when it happened. My mom was smart, he told me. My mom was intellectually curious. One of their first dates had been to see *A Clockwork Orange*, and she loved it. She wasn't put off by the violence at all. In fact, she was something of a true-crime junkie: Her favorite book was Mailer's *The Executioner's Song*. She wasn't big on music, though. That was a passion they didn't share. She fell asleep curled up in her seat when he took her to see Elvis Costello at the Orpheum Theater in Boston.

Mostly when my dad talked about my mom it was to remind me of my Jewish heritage. My dad converted to Judaism to marry my mom and he took it pretty seriously for a while, though after she died he never observed any kind of religious practice. He wasn't entirely sure he believed in God, and he'd been a good Irish Catholic growing up and going to Mass at St. Michael's in Providence. But he wanted me to understand the cultural importance of being Jewish, and I can only attribute this to how much it meant to my mom.

My grandmother and grandfather grew up in a time when being Jewish did not mean being white. Until the 1960s, when they moved from South Providence to Midland Drive in Cranston, they were, more or less, observant Jews. (Though my grandfather, after years of service in the military, quickly made it clear theirs would not be a kosher household. He cemented the deal by giving my grandmother her first bite of bacon.) My grandmother's married name was Goldman but her maiden name was Solinger and with her blue eyes and blond hair people told her all the time they were surprised to find she was a Jew. Why wasn't her nose bigger? Why didn't she smell weird, asked her childhood classmates.

They were a reform family, but celebrated the major holidays. What was most important to them was the culture. I've picked up the many Yiddish expressions that peppered my grandmother and grandfather's speech. Sometimes it's just the best way of explaining things. When I need to convey that something is a complete wreck, a disaster, a whole *thing*, it's easiest to just explain, "Oy gevalt, a total mishigas."

My dad made it clear, in the early years especially, that I'd go to the synagogue with my grandparents on the holidays, and even though he had no faith, I was born into one. In some sense I think my dad was proud of my Judaism. He equated it with intelligence, and nothing was more important to him than intelligence.

THERE'S A STORY that goes against the general mythology of my mom as a constant spritely ray of sunshine and maybe that's why I love it so much. On Midland Drive my mom had gotten into a screaming match with a neighbor—nobody can remember about what. She picked up a rock and threatened to hurl it at the neighbor. Somebody called the Cranston police. When the officer arrived he put my mom in the backseat of his cruiser and Brandy, the rangy mutt, my mom's fortuitous rescue dog, jumped inside with her and each time the officer approached the car to close the door Brandy let loose a fury of barking and growling. Over and over again, the officer tried to get back into his cruiser and over and over Brandy went wild. Eventually he shrugged. This was a neighborly dispute. He wasn't going to risk having his jugular ripped out because a small young woman refused to back down from an older male neighbor. Exhausted, patience spent, he told my mom to get out of the car. She did and Brandy hopped out behind her, docile as a doe but with a look in his eyes that warned everyone else from coming close. And that was that. That's the woman in the bottom photo, from the newspaper, I think. She was a force. "That dog was mean," my aunt said, "but he loved your mom."

———•———

MY MOM WAS also a drug addict. Specifically, she injected cocaine. She was in and out of rehab for many weeks at a time before I was born. But this aspect of her life was alluded to rarely in my family when I was growing up. My grandmother talked more about my mother's kindness, how she'd become friends with bad people and that was how she got into drugs. Bad Men. The Bad Men haunted my childhood. I had to be more careful than my mom was, my grandmother explained. Because my mom had been fearless and that had cost her her life. A little fear was a good thing. Don't put your trust in a Bad Man, she taught me.

———•———

THERE'S ANOTHER STORY about my mother's drug use that I've heard repeated in various forms. It's one of those things you look for: the repeating thing, the thing that after thirty years probably contains some nugget of truth, though it comes in different iterations, because at its heart it's the same story.

It involves my grandfather, my mother's father, whom she adored and who loved her back and who was completely broken by her murder. So this is not an origin story of blame but one of addiction, and opportunity, and war.

My grandfather, Louis Goldman, spent most of his childhood in the Jewish Home for Children, what would later become Miriam Hospital, in Providence, Rhode Island. By the time he was eighteen he was serving in World War Two. He met my grandmother at a USO dance in between his service in World War Two and his time in Korea. He was a cook, he played the bugle and the bagpipes, and he saw many, many people die.

Maybe my grandfather had post-traumatic stress disorder, or maybe he had that combined with some other form of mental illness, but he never held a steady job, refused to leave the house for years on end, and once had to be escorted, lying across the floor of the backseat of a police car, across the Newport Bridge because the drive over gave him a panic attack so severe he'd grasped his chest and cried, convinced he was having a heart attack.

And so my grandfather had pills. I remember the pills, lined up on the table by his reclining chair, his entire day spent organizing which pill came next. In the 1960s and early '70s, what would they have prescribed my big, tall grandfather, who was usually angry and filled at all times with a sense of terror? Seconal, maybe? Valium, certainly. And while my grandmother went to work each day in her neat blouse to keep the books at Klitzner Industries, my grandfather bought the groceries and he cooked all the meals, and he gave my mom some of his pills. Did my mom get high for the first time with her father? Some people insist upon it. They insist that he unwittingly got her hooked on something, that his collection of pills was a handy dispensary for my mom and that my grandfather gave her things to make her feel better because they made him feel better.

Maybe he said, "Calm down, Joanie. Have one of these." Or maybe he said, "Why do you look so tired, Joanie? Have one of these." But those who imply that my grandfather got my mom "hooked" clearly have no experience with the shrinking doom feeling of anxiety and depression, no experience with the power barbiturates and benzodiazepines hold, vise-like, over your body. They have no understanding of the way addiction exists, a little genetic blip in our DNA, and waits, waits, waits for an opportunity.

<hr />

AND THEN THERE were the photos. My mother carried a Canon AE-1 with her nearly everywhere. At some point in my childhood I came into possession of a green three-ring binder, dated 1978 to 1981, filled with hundreds of contact sheets and negatives developed by my mom in the darkroom she'd rigged up in the closet next to our small bathroom. Three years of her life documented through her eyes. How long did I hold on to that binder before I did anything with the negatives? It was years I think. And in a way, I'm glad I waited so long to have the negatives developed. I'm not sure I would have realized how much they say about her otherwise.

She photographed everything: her friends, children, birthday parties, weddings. She also went out on her own and photographed the things that interested her. There are rolls and rolls devoted to a union strike at the Institute for Mental Health. She also photographed Claus von Bülow's heavily publicized first trial for the attempted murder of his wife. In a state as small as Rhode Island, the von Bülow trial, and the national attention it brought, was practically legendary.

Claus was a Danish aristocrat and Sunny was an heiress and they lived with their children in the magnificent Newport mansion Clarendon Court. On the morning of December 22, 1980, Sunny was found unresponsive on her bathroom floor. She'd be in a coma for twenty-eight years before she finally passed away at the Mary Manning Walsh nursing home in New York. The prosecution argued that Claus had intentionally injected his hypoglycemic wife with insulin. Her death would have left him with twenty-one million dollars and the freedom to marry his mistress, soap opera actress Alexandra Moltke Isles. The defense argued that Sunny had overindulged in sweets and booze, celebrating the Christmas holidays, on the night she slipped into her long coma. Claus was found guilty and sentenced to thirty years in prison, a sentence that would be famously overturned by Alan Dershowitz a few years later.

I try to picture my mom there in the crush of the crowds and press with her camera. What was she hoping to see? Was she just fascinated by the spectacle? It's rare for Rhode Island to make the news, and when it does, everyone wants a part of it. The von Bülows would have been everything she was not: wealthy, cosmopolitan, and urbane.

Her favorite subjects by far were dogs, children, and my dad. She photographed my dad playing basketball. She photographed him playing softball for the *Providence Journal* team. She photographed a close-up of his flexed biceps. She photographed him lounging in a Burt Reynolds–style pose on a hammock; him sitting on the front steps of our house, a Chai, the Hebrew symbol for life, dangling from a chain around his neck. He would have been a compliant subject, my peacocking, handsome father with his thick black mustache and blue eyes. And she took more shots of him than she did of almost anybody else.

She took selfies as well, her Canon AE-1 set to self-timer as she lounged hand on her chin in a wicker rocking chair. She photographed herself photographing herself in the mirror. In my favorite picture, she doesn't get the shot quite right. She stands in front of the window of our living room in profile, naked, her belly round with me inside. Her head is cut off in the shot and she stands straight. She's documenting, not memorializing. "This is me, pregnant. This is how my body looks." It's late August 1980. She's twenty-six years old. She only has four years to live. My life has barely begun.

THREE

It feels like a long time, maybe a month after my mom disappears, that Dad picks me up at Grandma's house. He says we are going to build our own life together. I hug Dad, excited to be going with him. Grandma bends down and squeezes me, her smell of lipstick and Kleenex and clean hair all around us. "I love you," she says. "Be a good girl."

In the living room, I say good-bye to Grandpa. Spot perches on his lap and the two of them watch TV.

"Say bye to Spot," says Grandpa.

It feels okay to be leaving with Dad, but I'll miss Grandma and Grandpa. I don't want Dad to know, because I don't want him to feel bad, but he tells me, "You'll visit every Sunday. I promised your grandma."

I ask Dad, "Will Brandy and Ali come to Aunty Rita's with us?"

We are staying with Aunty Rita, Dad's sister, until we

find an apartment of our own. Dad had to give Brandy and Ali to a special farm for dogs who don't have homes, and when he tells me this he looks so sad I make a promise to myself I will never ask about them again.

Things are different at Aunty Rita's from the way they were at Grandma's house. Aunty Rita smokes like my mom did. Grandma, Grandpa, Aunty Sandy, and Dad all think smoking is disgusting, but Aunty Rita smokes long cigarettes that say VIRGINIA SLIMS in elegant green lettering up the side. In the mornings, Aunty Rita taps the end of her cigarette against the kitchen sink waiting for her coffee to brew. At night, she stirs dumplings into a pot of beef stew as she blows cigarette smoke into the air and drinks a glass of white wine.

Aunty Rita is so skinny that when she hugs me I feel her bones. I try not to squeeze too hard. She's short, like my mom, but Mom was round and full, and Aunty Rita is sharp and pointed. When she gets dressed in the morning she pulls her camisole against her chest, looking into the mirror of her vanity, and says, "Let's just hope you get boobies like your mom instead of nothing like me." I blush at the word *boobies* and look away but I like the way she lets me sit with her all the time and doesn't treat me like a little kid.

DAD ISN'T AROUND the house much because he works double shifts driving trucks for the *Providence Journal*, saving money for our apartment. He delivers both editions of the paper: the *Journal* in the morning and the *Evening Bulletin* at night. I think his job is glamorous, because the newspaper is famous. Once Dad shows me how he fills the honor box with newspapers and explains what it means: Only take one paper. On your honor.

He has a ring of keys with a key chain that is stamped EAST BAY DISTRIBUTION. The keys open all the honor boxes. We don't need a quarter to open them like everyone else, and Dad says we can have free newspapers whenever we want them.

When Dad leaves for work I'm afraid he will never come back. Sometimes when he leaves, I cry so hard I throw up, and Aunty Rita has to make a bed for me on the couch and put a wet washcloth on my forehead. We stay up late and watch movies in the dark living room, which feels special because I'm five years old and don't have a bedtime. All night I watch the glowing tip of my aunt's cigarette move up and down from the coffee table to her mouth. I fall asleep waiting for Dad to come home.

Sometimes, late at night, she offers me a sip of her Michelob Light, and tells me stories about her parents, my grandparents, who died before I was born. She tells me how much my dad loved my grandma, who died when he and Aunty Rita were still kids.

"Your dad and I are called Irish twins," she says. "Do you know what that means?"

I shake my head no.

"Irish twins is what they called us in school because we were born so close together we might as well be twins. We grew up together. That's why you two are here right now. Because I'll always take care of you."

Sometimes, when Dad doesn't have to work a day shift at the *Journal*, he lets me stay home from school. On the days when Dad and I stay home he says we are Being Bums. Being Bums involves eating oatmeal covered in sugar, so much sugar that it crunches with every spoonful. We take our oatmeal into Aunty Rita's living room and watch cartoons. My favorite cartoon is *Inspector Gadget*, and sometimes I talk to Dad pretending that my fingers are a phone, just like Gadget's. I pull out an imaginary antenna from my index finger and say, "Ring, Ring."

Dad pulls out his finger antenna and answers the phone.

"This is Inspector Gadget," I say.

"Can I talk to Leah?" asks Dad.

I say, "Hello, Dad, this is Leah."

Dad, still holding the imaginary phone to his ear, asks, "Did you tell Miss Razza that Mom was dead?" Miss Razza is my kindergarten teacher.

I look at Dad sitting at the other end of the plaid couch. There is a small mountain of pillows and blankets between us. I move my hand away from my face. I know Dad isn't playing the game anymore and I'm worried I'm in trouble.

"Did you say that?" he asks.

"Yes," I say.

"Why did you say that? What do you think happened to Mom?"

When I think of Mom I think of bones. She disappeared, and now she is dead.

"Do you want to know what happened to Mom?" he asks. "Mom died in a car accident," he says. "Do you understand what that means?"

I understand what a car accident means. I've seen them on television, and I've passed them on the side of the road so I understood the destruction and danger. I know Dad is lying but I'm not quite sure about what and because I love him and because he looks so sad, I decide to believe him.

"It means she's not coming back," I say.

Dad says, "It means we're our own family now."

———————

YEARS LATER, AFTER my mom and dad were both gone, I thought a lot about the family we never had. After so many secrets and silences I was determined to learn more about them. I wanted to find the truth. In college, in 2001, I searched the *Providence Journal* archives and came across an article about my mother's final moments. There was a description of her face turning purple as two men put all their strength into strangling her. At the time I was reading Yeats in one of my classes and I couldn't stop thinking about the poem "An Irish Airman Foresees His Death."

I know that I shall meet my fate
Somewhere among the clouds above;
Those that I fight I do not hate
Those that I guard I do not love;
My country is Kiltartan Cross,
My countrymen Kiltartan's poor,
No likely end could bring them loss
Or leave them happier than before.
Nor law, nor duty bade me fight,
Nor public man, nor cheering crowds,
A lonely impulse of delight
Drove to this tumult in the clouds;
I balanced all, brought all to mind,
The years to come seemed waste of breath,
A waste of breath the years behind
In balance with this life, this death.

It stayed with me because I associated it with my father, an Irishman, but as I read the vivid description of my mother's murder a feeling rushed through me. It was a kind of sick excitement. I was shaking a little bit in the computer lab at school as I read the article and kept thinking about one line from the poem. "A lonely impulse of delight..." That's how it felt to read those words for the first time.

And so I kept looking, for years, on and off, when the urge struck me.

I hunted down documents, collecting a larger and larger pile over the years. In one, a police report, a Cranston police officer writes that "On Friday 3-1-85 at approx. 1615 hours, I learned that the Providence PD had received an inquiry from Johnston PD in ref. to missing person, Joan B. Carroll 30 YOA. In checking with Johnston PD I was, in turn informed to contact Det. Donald Alberico of Prov. Intelligence Division. In attempting to do so, I spoke with Det. Francis Altomari who informed me that the body of Joan Carroll had been tentatively identified as being found in Sharon, MA."

It's unclear whether the police told my grandparents and aunt about the discovery of her body that evening. My grandmother insists that she heard about the body on the radio and my aunt insists she saw my mother's skeleton on the evening news, though it doesn't seem to make sense that the press would have known before them. She'd been missing six months. A young woman yes, but a drug addict also. Women "like that" often go missing. But when I continue to read the report, it states that the next morning, the officer responded to the Goldman home at 65 Midland Drive and spoke to both Mr. and Mrs. Goldman and their daughter in reference to the tentative identification of Joan Carroll. It was explained to them that the positive identification would not be able to be made until dental records had verified the same, but that they had good information to believe that the partially decomposed body of their daughter had been recovered in Sharon, Massachusetts.

Upon returning to hdqts, after notifying the Goldmans it was requested by Sgt Cooke that I call Det.

Thomas Oates and learn the further details of the recovery of the missing person. I learned that she had apparently been strangled in a motel in either North Attleboro or Attleboro prior to having her body dumped on the embankment of Rt. 95 in Sharon, Mass.

The next morning, 3-3-85, Hacket received confirmation of the dental records. And on 3-4-85 he cancelled the missing person report of Joan B. Carroll.

A photo of the girl was left with the OIC to be picked up by the Bristol County District Atty's office or by a representative of Mass. State Police in ref to their homicide. Cause of INC: Recovered body of missing person Joan B. Carroll. <<REPORT COMPLETED>>

When I read the report, I had that sick rush again. That "lonely impulse of delight." Here it was: the truth.

FOUR

I'm thrilled when my dad and I move out of Aunty Rita's and into our own apartment in a complex called Village Green. Mostly because I will have my own bedroom and Dad says we will get a kitten. We drive in through iron gates into a maze of gray-shingled buildings. We're apartment number 21, and have a numbered parking spot and mailbox with a lock and key. The best part about Village Green is the pool. In the summer Dad takes me swimming almost every day. He lies out on a chaise while I wear my body ragged swimming from one end to the other. I can't get enough of the deep chlorinated water, and Dad has to beg and bribe to get me out.

Dad makes me the same thing for lunch every time we go swimming: the Daddy Special, which consists of a can-shaped mound of tuna on a plate, no mayonnaise, and a pickle on the side.

In the mornings before he drops me off at school he asks, "What do you want to wear?" I am going through what my Aunty Sandy calls a princess phase, refusing to wear anything except party dresses, and then only if I'm also wearing a slip, stockings, and patent-leather shoes. Dad tries briefly to persuade me to put on a turtleneck under my dress. When I refuse, he doesn't fight me.

"What do you want for lunch?" he asks.

"Mustard sandwich," I say.

Dad spreads yellow mustard between two slices of white bread and cuts off the crusts. He opens a can of corned beef hash and fries it on the stove, spooning it onto a plate with a Little Debbie Oatmeal Creme Pie on the side. I love hash because it's what Dad ate in the army. We call it Vietnam Breakfast.

I look at the clock above the stove. I will be late for school. Dad will be late for work. But we don't care. In the apartment, Dad and I mostly keep our own time. I stay awake until midnight while Dad listens to records and drinks Heinekens. He tells me about fighting in Vietnam. I play jungle in my bedroom, crawling across the carpet on my elbows.

"Did we win the Vietnam War?" I ask.

"We won a lot of battles," Dad says.

"What does that mean?"

"It means the whole thing had no point, and a lot of people died."

"What was war like?" I ask.

"It rained a lot."

Dad wants me to know how important it is to be smart. Every night we take turns reading aloud to each other. In this way we get through *The Phantom Tollbooth, The Illustrated and Abridged David Copperfield, Of Mice and Men.* We read every single book by Roald Dahl. Dad tells me I'm so good at reading I will probably get an academic scholarship to Harvard one day and buys me a Harvard Crimson sweat suit.

At night, in my bedroom, I listen to the sounds of Dad in the rest of the apartment. I track his movements. If it's a good night, he laughs at something on the TV and rides the exercise bike in the living room and talks on the phone. If it's a bad night, the only thing I hear is the sound of Heineken cans as he drains and scatters them across the kitchen table, and the *glug-glug* of the Jameson as it pours from the bottle into an ice-filled glass. Or worse, there's the sound of Dad, assuming I'm asleep, slipping out the front door into the night. No matter how quietly he shuts and latches the metal door, the noise echoes in my head. When he comes back, hours later, I wake to half-remembered nightmares, sweating and nauseated. I wander into Dad's room.

"Can I sleep with you?" I ask. On these nights I crawl into his bed. He curls his giant body around mine. Sometimes he holds my hair to his face and weeps and mutters thick-sounding nonsense in his sleep. I think I would do anything to make him stop being sad.

Dad works at the *Providence Journal* offices at 75 Fountain

Street in Providence. The plaque on his desk says KEVIN CAR-
ROLL, DISTRIBUTION next to his electric typewriter. He has
a rolling office chair, like Dr. Claw, the faceless villain from
Inspector Gadget. I sit in the chair, my back to my dad, and
pretend to give evil orders.

Dad shows me where they make the newspaper: the
huge machines that cut the giant reams of paper and
print the words. In the middle of the machinery is a long
twisting slide where the finished and bundled newspapers
shoot down to the trucks for delivery. Every time I visit,
Dad asks if I want to go down the giant slide, and says
he'll do it with me. Every time I tell myself this will be the
visit I do it. I picture the truck drivers' faces, all my dad's
friends, when the two of us pop out the other end instead
of a bundle of newspapers. Every time I chicken out at the
last minute. The machinery is loud and metallic and the
slide seems too high.

At lunchtime we go to Murphy's Pub and Deli with all
of the guys from Dad's office. Murphy's is across the street
from the *Journal* office, tucked behind the hulking buildings of Westminster Street, shady and cool inside even
when the sun shines brightly. I love being at Murphy's
with Dad and his friends. Everything is a different shade
of green, from the felt coasters on the table to the wooden
bowl of pickled tomatoes and cucumbers that the waitress,
winking at Dad, slides in front of us.

"Cute date, Kev," she says.

"Marie, this is my daughter, Leah," he says, and reaches up to loop his arm lightly around her waist. My grandmother has told me how handsome Dad is, with his mustache and thick head of salt-and-pepper hair. Dad started to go gray in his early twenties but never tries to hide it. It's something that distinguishes him. He primps in front of every window, every mirror, smoothing back all his hair and saying, "Your dad is one good-looking man."

Even then I understand it to be a boast based on fact, something that is confirmed every time a woman laughs too loudly at one of his jokes and leans in to touch his arm, every time he walks into a room and smiles his big confident smile and everyone yells, "Kev!"

"Well look at you, Leah, with those beautiful brown eyes. Would you like a Shirley Temple?" Marie leans in close to me. Her hair brushes against my face and I smell her perfume. "Extra cherries?" Marie winks at me.

We eat corned beef sandwiches and potato salad. Dad and all his friends drink Heinekens and laugh. The men all call me Princess Leah, after the character from *Star Wars*, even though the pronunciation of my name is different. I love the nickname and the attention and the way that all the men laugh at Dad's jokes and tilt their heads to get the last drop of beer before they push their chairs away from the table and say, "Back to work!" Being inside Murphy's is like being inside the enormous belly of a friendly whale. Some of the men sway as we walk back to the *Journal*'s offices.

MURPHY'S TAVERN HAS moved locations since I went there as a child, but only a block and a half away. The interior is still brown and green; the pickled tomatoes and cucumbers are still at the ready. The owner, Ruth Ferrazano, rolls her eyes at this.

"I never thought my legacy would be pickles," she says.

I sit with Ruth at the corner of the long bar. The sun streaming in from the many windows (this incarnation of Murphy's is certainly brighter than the last) gives everything the impression of serenity. Even the old man with the oxygen tank at the other corner of the bar seems like a sweet old-fashioned mainstay. He makes polite conversation with the bartender, a friendly woman in her fifties with severe bangs. I sip slowly from a pint of Narragansett.

Downcity, as this part of Providence is known, is sedate, nearly silent. We are across the street from the convention center, but there is no convention. Up a few blocks is the Providence Civic Center, now called the Dunkin' Donuts Center. On the nights when the Providence Bruins play there, Ruth tells me, the bar can get pretty rowdy. The Providence police station, though, has moved across the 95 overpass. The *Providence Journal* headquarters are directly across the street, but the paper is a shell of its former self and the production facilities have long ago moved to a more industrial neighborhood. And so the bar is quiet, and peaceful. The oxygen tank hums slightly, or perhaps that is the air-conditioning. Ruth says, "I have to just tell you, you are very pretty. Your dad, my God, he was handsome."

There was a time when Murphy's was the second home not only to the guys from the *Journal*, but to the cops, the politicians from city hall, and various mafia types. "The mafia guys," says Ruth, "they left me pretty much alone."

"Do you know why?" I ask.

She shrugs. "Murphy's has always been kind of an icon. And I guess they just knew I didn't play that game. You know, don't get me wrong. We sold raffle tickets when we had to sell raffle tickets, but when it came down to it, I just didn't play the game, I guess. And they knew." It's not hard to imagine, looking at Ruth, that one would be disinclined to mess with her. Even against the backdrop of the deli case, of the silent shell of a city, she exudes a kind of sharp-edged elegance. A cook emerges from the kitchen to ask if he should put hot dogs on the board for the evening dinner specials. She stares at him for a beat and sighs slowly. "We talked about this, I think," she says.

"Oh yeah, yeah. I'm sorry, Ruth!" He rushes back into the kitchen.

Ruth turns to me. "This is my job? Hot dog patrol? I don't know what they would do if I wasn't here." Watching her hold court from the bar stool, I'm not sure either. She is the real thing. The old guard. This isn't the kind of woman who tells you that you are pretty to butter you up. She says it because you look like your father. And he was good people. And she says what she means.

"EVERYONE WAS JUST more fun back then," Ruth tells me. In the old days there were maybe four bars you went to: Player's Corner, Christopher's over on Pine Street, Gus Smith's, and Murphy's. In those days, the pressmen and the drivers at the *Journal* would all be done by two or three in the afternoon. They called Murphy's the Annex.

"In a lot of ways," says Ruth, "the *Journal* made Murphy's a success." But it wasn't just *Journal* guys. At Murphy's you could sit down next to a Supreme Court judge having a beer on his lunch break. A gangster would gladly sit next to a union guy. There would be a table of cops two seats over.

"Paolino would be here at the same time as Cianci," Ruth tells me of the rival ex-mayors of the city. In his last days of freedom, before he was sent off to prison, indicted on the RICO statute—the Racketeer Influenced and Corrupt Organization Act signed into law in 1970 and used extensively to bring down the bosses of the Italian mafia—Buddy Cianci would walk down from the Biltmore Hotel, where he lived in a suite, and sit at a table by the deli, order a pastrami on pumpernickel cut into fours, and say his good-byes to a processional of people from every corner of the city who came to join him for a few minutes at a time. Nobody minded that the charge he'd been convicted of essentially stated that he'd run the city of Providence as a criminal enterprise for his own financial gain. People loved the short portly man in the black toupee who traveled around the city with a stash of his own brand of marinara sauce to hand out as gifts. They'd already reelected him once, after his first criminal conviction while in office, that one an assault. I still own a black T-shirt, now wearing a bit at the seams, that shows the former's mayor's smiling face and the declaration, FREE BUDDY!

"They say Hasbro is moving into the old Blue Cross Building," Ruth tells me. "That will be good for this part of the city. And with the Convention Center...you never know." An older woman wearing an apron appears next to us bearing a small dish of sliced olives. "Ruth," she asks, "I thought we weren't going to open these?"

Ruth sighs heavily. "Of course not," she says. "You know there's a picture of them right on the side of the can. You don't have to be psychic to tell they're not whole olives." She waves her hand. "Forget it. We'll use them in a salad or something." She turns to me and shakes her head.

———•———

AFTER WE MOVE into the apartment, Dad starts to have girlfriends. There's Gail, a photographer at the *Journal*. She has a full head of unruly blond curls and doesn't seem as pretty as Mom, but she laughs all the time and says things that make Dad laugh, and I like her. There's Kathleen with the long black hair and I think she is beyond glamorous. He meets Ann-Marie at Giant Steps, the small private school I attend along with her son, Derek, who is my age. My teacher Miss Razza is always yelling at Derek and making him stand in the corner, not like Gregory Calderiso who has handsome brown eyes and is good at vocabulary. I'd invited Gregory to my fifth birthday and kissed him on the lips in my bedroom closet, telling him, "Pretend I'm She-Ra and you're He-Man."

I sleep over at Ann-Marie's house a lot while Dad goes out. She lets me take long bubble baths and then wear her silky nightgowns, the straps held up with a barrette fastened between my shoulder blades. She brushes and blow-dries my long hair, and when I look at myself in the mirror, I can't stop admiring how clean I am, how shiny my hair looks, how nice I smell. Dad uses Denorex shampoo and Irish Spring soap at home, so usually I smell like that. Ann-Marie, though, has what seems like hundreds of different bottles, all filled with soap, shampoo, and bubble bath. Her bathroom is like a pharmacy of pink lotions and gels.

At night Derek and I fight over who gets to sleep on the couch. Ann-Marie blows up an air mattress and sets it up in the living room, right outside her bedroom door. Derek and I compromise by sleeping on it together beneath a brown blanket, decorated with a jungle scene. I get to sleep beneath the lion part of the blanket.

Because I stay over at Ann-Marie's house so much, I see less of Grandma. When I do go there she asks me about Dad's new girlfriend.

"This Mary-Anne," she says, "you like her? She's nice to you? You like her son?" I answer yes to all of Grandma's questions and try again and again to correct her about the name.

"It's Ann-Marie," I say.

"Oh, I know, I know," says Grandma as she hunts around the kitchen for a scrap of paper to write the name down on. Grandpa never asks about Ann-Marie or Dad. He asks a lot about school and laughs when I tell him about how smart I am and all the books I can read. He tells me how smart my mom was, and how much she read. He says I'm just like her.

When Grandma leaves for work, Grandpa and I make lunch and give Spot his heart medicine. Grandpa hides the pills inside a Saugy and even then Spot sometimes eats the whole thing and leaves the pill, licked clean, on the kitchen floor. Grandpa pulls another Saugy from the big boiling pot, covers it in yellow mustard and celery salt, and serves it to me on a slice of bread. I like Saugy's better than regular hot dogs, because the skin snaps when you bite into one.

But it is still Dad I like being with the best. When I'm alone with him I feel special and safe and like nothing bad could happen to either of us. At the grocery store I ride on his shoulders, up so high that when I look down I get a swooning feeling. Instead I look straight ahead and pretend I am as tall and strong as Dad. I know all the other kids in the market are jealous of the way I sit above them like a queen.

Dad tells me stories about when he was a kid. He says he was bad and got into lots of fights. He shows me how the fingers on his right hand are all bent. He says, "I know how to fight and I'll always protect you."

Sometimes we pretend we are in the WWF, and Dad pile-drives me into his waterbed. "Body slam next!" I scream. I love the feeling of flipping through the air knowing Dad will catch me at the last second. "Now a clothesline!"

Dad plays softball for the *Providence Journal* team and I sit in the bleachers with the wives and the other kids. He hits the ball hard and runs as fast as he can. Once he slides into third and I hear another player say, "Man you gotta watch out for that Kenny Rogers–looking moth- erfucker." I know he's talking about my dad's gray hair and mustache, and the wives around me slap their knees and elbow each other. When dad gets back to the dugout he downs a Heineken and gives everyone high fives, and when the game is over, the *Journal* wins and Dad picks me up to take me to the car and I can tell everyone is looking at us because he's the best at everything.

———————

MY DAD AND Ann-Marie get married in the living room of my new grandmother's house. Ann-Marie wears a beaded white cashmere sweater and knee-length white skirt. Dad wears a suit, like usual. He looks like he's going to work. Derek and I watch from the dining room table where I eat cube after cube of cheese from the appetizer platter until my stomach hurts. When the ceremony is over Aunty Rita hugs Dad and then whispers into Ann-Marie's ear, "I hope you know what you got yourself into." When Dad and

Ann-Marie get back from their honeymoon, Ann-Marie has a deep tan and her hair is pulled back in a tight French braid.

"Why do you look like that?" I ask.

Dad's ruddy skin looks the same to me, but Ann-Marie's new bronze skin makes me uncomfortable. It's like she married my dad and came back a new person. She brings back gifts from Mexico: a pink shirt with palm trees and rhinestones, a set of maracas, and a small doll with black hair and a brightly patterned dress. I put them in a bottom drawer of my dresser.

Dad brings back a dinosaur poster from the Smithsonian, where they'd gone on a layover. I love it because it shows eight different kinds of dinosaurs and each one is labeled. He also brings me a fossil of a trilobite. I hold it and trace the ancient bug with my fingers, trying to comprehend how old it really is.

We move to a new apartment in Village Green, toward the fancier part of the development. We have a new pool, but we move in winter and it's covered over. I'm excited because we have two floors and my upstairs room overlooks the edge of Village Green where the landscaping stops and the brambles and woods take over.

When the weather starts to warm up Dad takes me to the Looff Carousel in Riverside. The carousel is the only thing left from what was once a grand amusement park on Narragansett Bay. In addition to its hand-carved wooden horses, the carousel has dragons, tigers, zebras, and ornately carved benches to ride on. Dad says it's a work of art. He parks himself on one of the benches that line the outer building as I go around and around. I look for him during each revolution; he's there with his arms crossed and his legs splayed out in front of him, the newspaper folded at his side. I've just read the Chronicles of Narnia and like to pretend that the animals on the carousel are part of a massive parade of majestic talking animals. We're celebrating a great victory over evil, marching toward home.

There's a man who dispenses metal rings with the aid of a long wooden extension. You're meant to reach from your perch and grab a hold of a ring as you spin past. If you catch a brass one you get a free ride. Every time we drive to the carousel I tell Dad that today will be the day I reach out and grab the ring, but when the time comes I'm always too afraid to extend my body and reach out. I don't trust that I won't fall from the horse and get caught up in the ancient-looking cogs that power the ride. Derek once grabbed the brass ring and Dad high-fived him and let us both go around another three times.

This day, though, Derek isn't with us. It's just Dad and me. When I'm done on the carousel, we buy popcorn from the old-timey-looking vendor and walk down to the water. I love the carousel, but sometimes it also makes me sad. A long time ago it had been glamorous, but now it seems very old.

Dad holds my hand while we walk. "I think it would be good," he says, "for our new family if you start thinking of Ann-Marie as your new mom. I think your real mom would have wanted you to do that."

It sounds like he practiced this, and I can tell how important it is. "But won't my real mom see me from heaven?" I ask. "Won't she get mad if she thinks I want someone else to be my mom?"

"No," says Dad. "I think your mom would want us all to be happy in our new family." He hugs me around the neck and pulls me close to him as we walk. "And it would make me happy if you think of Ann-Marie as your new mom. Will you do that for me?"

I nod yes. Of course I will. Of course.

FIVE

When I was living alone in the apartment with my dad we had a framed print of the iconic Maxell ad known as the Blown Away Guy. I was sure that was *my* dad's martini swept up in the audio tempest, *my* dad's tie thrashing behind him. The lush-haired guy in the ad for Maxell cassettes getting blasted by the music coming from a pair of JBL speakers, the veritable image of cool: It was Kevin Carroll. I was certain.

The Blown Away Guy was aspirational, and my dad aspired. He might not have known that the Blown Away Guy's chair was designed by Le Corbusier, or maybe even who Le Corbusier was, but he knew what could make a guy eschew a savings account in favor of a McIntosh 2105 receiver for the baddest hi-fi in town. He might not have known not to douse himself in so much Polo cologne that when he left a room you could still smell him in the air, but he knew how to rock a pin-striped suit and red suspenders and make it work. And when my dad strutted into the production facility at the *Providence Journal* he was the best-dressed guy there. Of course, he was the only guy in a suit; these guys were driving trucks to deliver the paper. But it didn't matter. He looked good. And he knew it. Everyone did.

My dad was a certain kind of guy. He dropped out of high school in the tenth grade to enlist in the army. He wasn't a patriot—he was a bored seventeen-year-old who didn't get along with his father and stepmom. But he was, as one of his co-workers at the *Journal* told me years later, in a letter, "so smart it was spooky."

———◆———

WHEN WE DIE we leave behind a paper trail, and I started collecting my father's life as it appeared on paper, just as I had been doing with my mother's. I have twenty years' worth of my dad's personnel records from the *Journal*, charting his move from mail clerk to manager of distribution. In 1982 he handwrote a cover letter:

Sir:

I would like to enter my name in consideration for the supervisory positions posted in the mailing room. I am 31 years old, married, and the father of a two year old.... Since working at the *Journal* I feel that I have compiled an excellent work and attendance record. I am also in excellent condition and shape. I feel the time is right for me to assume new responsibilities and challenges.

Thank you, Kevin Carroll.

I have his war record. At seventeen, he was only five foot ten and barely 160 pounds, not yet the solid man he'd become, but it was 1968 and they took him gladly. Initially he signed up for airborne duty but changed his mind. As part of the Nineteenth Combat Engineer Battalion he spent most of his time as a company clerk and his last two months as a demolition specialist, clearing the roads of mines every morning. A friend's father, an army officer, translated the jargon of the records for me. He ended his note of explanation by saying, "I don't know the rest of the story, Leah, but for those three years of his life, your Dad's service records paint him as an exemplary young man."

I have his autopsy report: "At autopsy, he had an enlarged greasy liver with steatohepatitis, consistent with acute and chronic ethanol use, as well as an enlarged heart with microscopic findings consistent with hypertensive cardiovascular disease. An additional significant contributing condition to his death included chronic obstructive pulmonary disorder."

I have various notes he wrote me throughout the years. One is from when I was a teenager and is typed out. I can no longer remember the context but he writes, "I Leah's father do promise to be more fatherly and help Leah through this difficult period she is experiencing. I further give Leah free notice to ask me about any subject without any fear of anger on my part. Should I break this contract at any time, I encourage Leah to bring it out and show it to me and put me in my place. This I do promise as Leah's dad, because I love her and because she is the light of my life."

I have the note he wrote me on the night before he died, also typed and printed. "Please don't be mad," it begins. "Alcoholism and depression have ruined my life."

But still it is almost as hard to explain him as it is to explain my mom, whom I never really knew. I feel like I'll never get it right. How you couldn't trust him, not for a minute, but you always did. How when he turned his attention to you it was like everything was lit up, and when he decided he was done everything went ice-cold. The way that he presented himself as invincible: smarter, faster, funnier, so that when he was vulnerable it was somehow extra pitiful. The way he scrunched up his chin and poked it with his index finger when he was thinking and didn't realize anyone was looking. The ways he let me down, and I let him down, and how I still think about him, twenty years later, almost every day.

There were these specifics: He took road trips to Civil War battlefields. He was a heavy hitter on the *Journal*'s softball team. He said the best band he ever saw live was Television. He took me to the Holocaust Museum and to

my first sushi restaurant, and sometimes we would drive to
New York and take photos for the whole day and then drive
back the three hours to Rhode Island. He was Irish Ameri-
can and hated, in roughly descending order: Margaret
Thatcher, Ronald Reagan, and Morrissey. He blasted solo
Lindsey Buckingham and Parliament Funkadelic from his
JBL speakers so loud that our little apartment shook.

Our print of the Blown Away Guy hung above a bust of
Beethoven, which in turn sat atop an antique wooden con-
sole radio. Beethoven was a little taller than my eye level
and sometimes I pretended the bust was the head, and the
radio was his body, and the whole thing was my boyfriend.
Blown Away Guy and Beethoven were the sole decorative
objects in that apartment as far as I recall. When I asked
Dad if he was the guy in the photo, if he was the cool guy
in the sunglasses drinking a martini with the volume up
extra high, he just laughed like he had a secret. At some
point, in the way a kid learns what money does, or over-
hears an old lady swear, I came to understand that the guy
in the picture was some other man, a model. But that was
just a pointless detail.

———◦———

I'M EIGHT YEARS old when Dad tells me we have to have
a Serious Talk. He sits on the floor of my bedroom and
before he has a chance to say anything, I ask him, "Are you
going to tell me my mom was murdered?" I have no idea
where the knowledge came from. It was just there. For

years I've been telling people my mom died in a car accident, just like Dad told me at Aunt Rita's. But deep inside,
I've always known the truth. It's just been in there, waiting,
and finally saying it out loud feels good. But Dad tells me
that her murder is something we have to keep a secret.

"It's personal," he tells me. "It's something we don't talk
about outside of the family, okay?"

I keep a picture of Mom in my dresser, an eight-by-ten
she'd developed herself, and I sometimes take it out of the
drawer and study it. I think about how she will never look
any different to me than she does in this photo. I think about
it for a long time and stare at the picture, and when I try to
picture my mom in my head, it's only the face and pose from
the photograph that I see. I'm forgetting the real her.

The word *murder* feels like a bad word, like something
to be ashamed of. I don't want anybody to think bad things
about my mom and so I continue telling people she died in
a car accident. After our Serious Talk, Dad and I never talk
about the way she died again.

THIS, I NOW know, are the details of how my mother
died:

On October 18, 1984, she attended services at Temple
Sinai with my grandmother. Then she said she was going
to meet a friend named Debbie. Really, she was on her
way to Sonny Russo's Restaurant in Johnston, Rhode
Island. Sonny Russo's was where Gerald Mastracchio Sr.

conducted much of his criminal business. It was where my mom, who just a few months prior had completed a rehabilitation program that did not take, knew she could get drugs.

That night, October 18, the men happened to be talking about a girl they knew, Joanie, or Joanie the Jew, as they called her sometimes, alias Joanie Grant, real name, Joan B. Carroll. The men were discussing how Joanie "had to go." And when she walked into the restaurant, Mastracchio said, "This is beautiful."

He invited her to party; promised her drugs. She told him she had to go home, attend to personal matters, check on her child. They made a date for later that night.

When she returned she parked her car around the corner and left with Gilbert and Mastracchio to rent a hotel room in Attleboro, Massachusetts, just over the Rhode Island line. They all shot up cocaine. Mastracchio appeared from the bathroom holding a wet towel and started to strangle her. Her legs went out from under her and as she struggled, Mastracchio yelled for Gilbert to help him. As her face turned purple, Gilbert stepped on one end of the towel for leverage and Mastracchio said, "Come on, you rat, give me the death rattle." Then, when she was finally dead, they wrapped my mom's body in a blanket, put it in the trunk of the car, and drove off, pulling eventually to the side of I-95 where they left her body in a marshy area off the exit ramp. She'd officially be a missing person. For the next six months.

⎯⎯•⎯⎯

I wonder sometimes what she must have been thinking as these two men choked her to death. I think most of all she must have been confused. Why was this happening?

⎯⎯•⎯⎯

This is why my mother was killed:

On September 7, 1984, the Rhode Island State Police raided Mastracchio Sr.'s home. They found weapons, drugs, syringes, and money. They found the heart of Rhode Island's drug trade. They arrested everyone on site. One of the men arrested that day was taken into the state police barracks where he was handcuffed to a desk for hours awaiting intake. As he sat there, waiting, the man realized that a detective had left the affidavit in support of the search warrant for the raid on the desk to which the man was chained. So he reached out, cuffs and all, and read every single page.

When given his one phone call, he used it to dial Mastracchio Sr. and tell him everything he'd just read in the affidavit: There was a confidential informant. That person had given details about Mastracchio's apartment including the fact that the street-facing windows were made of one-way glass. Mastracchio Sr. was furious. He liked to say that he valued loyalty above all. My mom had recently made a comment to him about the mirrored glass, something

like, "Oh you can see in, but you can't see out." That was
enough evidence for him.

"Joanie's a rat," Mastracchio said. "I'll kill her with my
bare fucking hands."

———————

AFTER MY MOTHER was murdered she likely might have
remained a missing person forever, but on February 28,
1985, the Providence Police raided Peter Gilbert's home in
a drug bust.

In custody at the Providence police station Gilbert told
the two police detectives guarding him that he felt like he
was having a heart attack. In the ambulance on the way
to Miriam Hospital, he told the detectives he had information on three murders and some other crimes and he'd
tell them whatever they wanted, he promised, if they gave
him protection from Mastracchio. He said he'd bring the
police to the bodies. And there was more. Gilbert swore
that the drug dealing, the robberies, and the murders to
which he would confess were condoned and sanctioned by
the man running organized crime in Rhode Island, Raymond Patriarca.

Patriarca had been New England's most powerful organized crime boss for more than three decades and tying him
directly to a crime would advance the careers of everyone
involved—the arresting officers, the entire Providence Police
Department, and especially the attorney general, an incum-
bent Republican and former nun named Arlene Violet.

In fact, Violet had run for her office on a platform largely devoted to the promise that she would bring down the mafia in Rhode Island. On the night that Gilbert started talking Violet, along with the specially created Intelligence Bureau of the Providence police, couldn't resist the opportunity for a possible RICO indictment against the Patriarca crime family.

By ten thirty on the night of his arrest, Gilbert had given detailed information about three murders and the robbery of a liquor store that he claimed were linked to the Patriarca crime family. The next day the office of the attorney general dispatched a representative to make a deal. If Gilbert told them everything he knew, and if he could link his crimes to the Patriarca crime family by testifying in court, he'd be given a sentence of forty years—thirty suspended and ten years to be served in the custody of a fledgling state Witness Protection Program. If all went according to the deal, he'd never spend a day in an actual prison.

On March 1, 1985, Gilbert brought the police to my mother's skeletal remains off the side of the highway in Sharon, Massachusetts. He confessed to the murder of Joe West, who'd been found dead in a parked car, shot in the head execution style, a few months before. Gilbert then helped the police track down the remains of Joseph Olivo, another drug customer who Mastracchio and Gilbert had suspected was an informant.

Olivo's dismembered torso was found, with Gilbert's guidance, under two thousand pounds of refuse in the local landfill. In grand jury testimony, Gilbert would later explain that he couldn't recall exactly where all the other pieces of Olivo had gone, but he was sure he'd thrown the man's legs in a dumpster outside of a Mister Donut franchise in Cranston.

All three victims were young drug users. The decision to make a deal with Gilbert was a simple one for the state of Rhode Island: a few dead addicts in exchange for the RICO indictment they'd been seeking for decades against the Patriarca crime family?

By their logic, it was a deal they'd be foolish to turn down.

———◆———

SIX

Ann-Marie and Dad decide to move to Barrington when Derek and I are entering third grade. It's where Ann-Marie grew up, and while it's only ten minutes away and one town over, it seems like another world to me. In Barrington we will have a house with our own yard. In Barrington, the schools are the best. In Barrington, we will be a happy family, the four of us with our dog and our house and our excellent schools. Nobody needs to know that Ann-Marie is my stepmom and Derek is my step-brother and that Dad comes home late at night or not at all, angry, and sad, and happy, and silly, and mean all at once. Barrington is where we will start over, officially.

Dad tells me that Barrington is full of rich people, that it's the richest town in Rhode Island. When we look for houses with the Realtor, Dad says, "We're off to Baaaar-ington," dragging out the *a* and keeping his jaw locked.

Dad is from South Providence, the toughest part of Rhode Island. He grew up on Eddy Street in a three-family-style house on the first floor with his mother and father, Aunty Rita, and my Uncle Tommy who I've only met once.

My grandparents on Dad's side died when he was still young—his mom when he was thirteen and his dad when he was eighteen. He doesn't say many nice things about his father and almost never talks about his mother. Aunty Rita tells me that while their mom lay dying of liver failure in Rhode Island Hospital, she'd been comatose and unresponsive for days until Dad rode his bike to the hospital. She woke up just long enough to tell him she loved him and then slipped back into a coma and died the next day. Dad was her baby, Aunty Rita says, her favorite, and it was much worse for him to have lost his mom when he was older than it has been for me, because he will remember her for the rest of his life, and I will eventually forget my mom entirely.

Sometimes, on the way back from Grandma Ruth's house, Dad jumps off the highway and we drive through South Providence. The house he grew up in is now a vacant lot. He says a "firebug" had burned it down.

"What's a firebug?" I ask.

"An arsonist," he says. "Someone who sets a fire to see all the fire trucks come and put it out."

"Was it scary?" I ask. "Growing up here?"

Dad shakes his head. "It wasn't scary," he says. "It was different from Baaaarington."

Barrington is a lot like how Dad promises it will be. It's

quiet and idyllic with neatly trimmed front yards, Little League games, and even an eighteenth-century clapboard church topped with a white steeple. There are boats anchored along the Barrington River, and a little beach with access to Narragansett Bay. The best thing, I think, about Barrington is that it's a "dry" town. You can't legally buy or serve alcohol within the town limits. I've recently been told what I already realized—that when Dad comes home late at night acting strangely, it's because he's drunk. To me, a dry town seems like the answer to our prayers. It's a place to really become a family.

Ann-Marie tells us that technically, we live in West Barrington, not Barrington proper. Years ago, the town had two post offices and two zip codes, but while the post office is gone, the division is still there in spirit. The western side is more modest; there are small streets and lots of construction from the 1960s, and smaller, one-level houses like ours. On the other side the houses are much older, some hundreds of years old, and the yards are bigger. There are many commanding two-story homes with semicircle driveways and pools in the backyard. The epitome of Barringtonian opulence is Rumstick Drive. These houses along Narragansett Bay have huge glass windows overlooking lawns filled with ancient green trees. There are kayaks lashed to the Volvos in the driveways, and ski racks on the roofs of the Mercedes.

We drive down Rumstick Drive and I imagine what it would be like to live in one of those beautiful homes. I imagine having a four-poster bed and taking horseback riding lessons. I'd want Dad to be just the same: funny, and smart, and handsome, except he'd never drink and instead would come to watch me play sports like soccer. In real life I've never even tried to play soccer.

Dad learned to take pictures from my mom and over the years it has become his passion. Our house is filled with camera equipment: tripods, giant lenses, issues of *Shutterbug* and *Popular Photography*. Dad has Derek and me sit for his photo experiments. We make a sad face on one side of the couch and then a happy face on the other for a double exposure. He has Derek leap from a tree and tries to capture his movement frame by frame.

Dad never goes anywhere without a successive series of Canon cameras hanging from his chest and a giant camera bag overflowing with filters and flashes and lenses stuffed beneath the passenger-side seat of his car. Dad's cameras are large and expensive and draw the attention of people wherever we go.

"Are you a photographer?" people ask as he sets up the camera on the tripod at Barrington Beach.

"Yeah," he tells them. "Do you take pictures?"

"Oh no, no," they answer, looking admiringly at the complicated setup he has rigged to capture the sunset over the gentle waves of the bay. "Where do you work?"

"The *Providence Journal*," Dad answers and begins clicking away, while I stand beside him, fetching items from his camera bag the way a nurse might fetch scalpels for a surgeon, and busting with pride. Because it *is* true that Dad is a photographer, and it *is* true that he works at the *Providence Journal*, and if the guy asking the questions goes away thinking that Dad is a photographer for the *Providence Journal*, that's fine with Dad and me. We don't have to explain ourselves.

Derek and I enter the third grade at Primrose Hill Elementary. The elementary schools in Barrington go to the third grade, and after that you move on to middle school, so the third graders are the oldest kids at Primrose. Ann-Marie makes sure that Derek and I aren't in the same class, so we won't spend too much time together and fight. Mr. Waugh teaches my class. He has an adopted son that he talks about all the time. He tells us that because his son is adopted he gets to have two birthdays: the day of his actual birth and the day of his adoption. I think it would be strange to have a father who teaches elementary school and once I have a nightmare that Dad is teaching my third-grade class and being nice to all of the other kids. I wake in a sweating, jealous fury.

When school gets out, Derek and I go to the after-school program at the YMCA to wait for Ann-Marie to pick us up on her way home from Blue Cross/Blue Shield, where she works in the claims department. The counselors try to engage us in some physical activity in those few hours between school and home. While most of the other kids play basketball and kickball, I sit in the rec room reading

Baby-Sitters Club books and weaving and unweaving pot-holders on a plastic loom, dodging all attempts the counselors make at getting me to participate.

I can't wait for Ann-Marie to come get us at the end of the day. In the winter it's dark when I finally see her head in the high window of the hallway outside the basement room, her short hair permed and moussed, colorful earrings dangling at the sides of her face as she walks. I envy her dangly earrings fiercely, and she tells me that she'll convince Dad to let me wear them. Settling into the front seat of her car on the way home from the YMCA I balance the small shopping bag containing her heels and Tupperware in my lap. She presses down on the gas pedal with her sneakered foot, tugging at a run in her pantyhose and slaps Derek's hand away from the radio.

Because Ann-Marie works all day, the food she makes for dinner is always fast and easy. I'm a picky eater and bargain every night about how many more bites I have to take. We eat bowls of egg noodles with sirloin tips and peas, chicken thighs covered in cream of mushroom soup and canned green beans, and in the summer, corn on the cob and instant mashed potatoes. Though we eat as a family, we rarely speak during meals, and once we're done eating Dad wanders away from the table and back into the bedroom to sleep, leaving his empty plate on the table.

"Good job on dinner, Ann-Mo," he'll yell from the hallway.

There are many nights dad leaves the house and I ask him where he's going.

"Out," he always says. These are the nights he comes home late and wakes up me and Derek to arm-wrestle. It starts out fun but then sometimes he let us win and then tells us he's pathetic and makes us say it back to him. Whenever he tells me he's going "out," I get a sick worried feeling, and on one of those nights I go into their bedroom where Ann-Marie is on the bed watching television.

"What if Dad gets killed by the serial killer?" I ask.

"What serial killer?"

"The New Bedford Serial Killer!" I say. "They can't find him and he might kill Dad."

In 1988 there is a serial killer dropping the bodies of the women he kills off a stretch of highway in nearby New Bedford, Massachusetts. My mind is consumed by this story, fed by the television shows I watch with Ann-Marie all the time: *A Current Affair, Unsolved Mysteries, Sally Jessy Raphael,* and *Oprah.* It seems just as likely to me that Dad will walk out the door and be killed by the New Bedford Serial Killer as it does that he'll come home late, stumbling and drunk.

"Your dad will be fine," says Ann-Marie. "He always is."

She sees I'm still scared and sighs. "Don't worry," she says. "That serial killer only kills women, so your dad is safe." I feel sorry for those women, but that fact helps put my mind at ease once I know Dad is not a target.

In April 2015, I sit in a small private room in the medium-security section of the Rhode Island Adult Correctional Institution. On one side of me is the prison's PR representative, and on the other is Gerald Mastracchio Jr. He has been in prison most of his life. As a teenager, Junior murdered a thirteen-year-old boy by beating him and throwing his unconscious body off the Jamestown Bridge. As a slightly older teenager he joined his father in the Rhode Island drug trade. A little after that, his father, Gerald Mastracchio Sr., murdered my mother.

Junior has agreed to see me, to answer my questions. He says he hopes he can provide some closure. He's clean-shaven. He has a chubby, pleasant face and a small smattering of jailhouse tattoos. The smell of his sweat fills the small room. At my request, Junior reminisces a bit about his dad, who died in 2000. He tells me that in the 1970s Junior's mom would drop him off at the maximum-security wing of the ACI to visit with his father, and as a little boy he'd hang out in the jail's garage with an inmate who washed the state vehicles and was serving time for killing his wife, mother-in-law, sister-in-law, and their dog. Sometimes the inmate stopped cleaning the cars for a bit to take Junior frog hunting in the muddy patch behind the garage.

"I'd never seen prison as a bad thing because when I did go in and visit my father, the prison system was different," he says. "Inmates pretty much did what they wanted. I'd go in there and there'd be candy and cookies and milk and playing games. That's pretty much all I'd seen in the gangster type of people. They're all shaking hands and all that good stuff."

———•———

HIS FATHER WAS a career criminal. Mastracchio Sr.'s adult police record begins in 1943, when he assaulted a Providence police officer. There were other convictions: attempted rape, assault with intent to rob, assault with a deadly weapon, and in 1969 a second-degree murder charge for shooting a guard during a holdup of the Hood milk plant in Providence.

"I remember going to visit my dad and saying, 'Hey, I need a place to get pot.' The following weekend when I went to see him he gave me a name and an address. I went up to Coventry and met this gentleman who opened up a barn and had bales of marijuana for seventy-five dollars a pound. It was like, 'Here you go, kid. Take what you want.' That's how I got stuck. My father was in jail. I guess I was sixteen. My father overturned his sentence and got out. Then we used to have Sundays at my aunt's house or my grandmother's house."

Between Sunday dinners, father and son decided to really get into the drug business. They had a connection in New York, and had the best heroin in Rhode Island, all the cocaine they wanted, and as many narcotics in pill form as a pharmacy. Eventually they needed to bring on other guys—mostly prison buddies of Gerry Sr. There was Kevin Hanrahan, Bobby Almonte, Richie Gomes ("Richie started out as John Gotti's driver in New York. He was kicked out in New York because he wouldn't leave the cocaine alone," says Gerry Jr.), and a newer guy, a guy who'd given Gerry Sr. an alibi once: Peter Gilbert. Just a few years after earning Mastracchio Sr.'s trust and becoming his right-hand man in the drug ring, Gilbert would help murder my mom—an act he'd tell authorities had the blessing and protection of Raymond Patriarca.

And now, three decades after this all happened, Gerry Jr. puffs out his chest at the mention of Patriarca, and at the insinuation that I'm trying to get him to admit his own drug dealing was sanctioned by the New England mob, as the attorney general of Rhode Island would later contend. He may be a killer, he may be a thief and a drug dealer and a liar, but he is no rat.

"It didn't have anything to do with Raymond," Junior says. "I do not glorify my dad or brag about him. The reality was my father was a vicious person." Then, with barely a pause, he tells me, "But he was the nicest guy in the world."

———◦———

RAYMOND PATRIARCA WAS a legend in Rhode Island, a state founded by Roger Williams, a man who, depending on your viewpoint, was either a religious zealot who'd been kicked out of the Massachusetts Bay Colony, or a remarkably forward-thinking leader who advocated for the separation of church and state and respect for the Native Americans before anyone else. Rhode Island was the first colony to renounce the British Crown and the last to ratify the US Constitution; it was a state that was heavily involved in the African slave trade but abolished racial segregation in schools in the 1800s, and a state that had, until very recently, a law that made prostitution legal provided it took place indoors. In this state, Raymond Patriarca was an icon. He was something that made Rhode Island matter.

Born in 1908, he was in prison by 1928 for breaking and entering, and by the 1930s he was called Rhode Island's Public Enemy Number One. In 1938 he was back in prison for a robbery in Massachusetts, but was pardoned just three months later by the Governor's Council. "I guess the board just had the Christmas spirit," he told a reporter. Later, Patriarca would insist, "I was a bootlegger. I was a gambler. But since I got out of prison in 1945, I've done nothing wrong." That's when some people started calling him "the mayor of Providence."

For the last half of his life, Patriarca controlled the world of organized crime in New England. He answered directly to the "five families" of New York and was in charge of Rhode Island, New Hampshire, Maine, Massachusetts, and parts of Connecticut. He was Gennaro Angiulo's boss, the infamous Boston underboss brought down by RICO in the early 1980s by a series of FBI wiretaps and, most agree, tips from rival Boston gangster Whitey Bulger.

Patriarca operated his business out of an innocuous storefront for the National Cigarette Service, a vending machine company located on Federal Hill, the Italian section of Boston. From inside the little building, known as "the Office," Patriarca oversaw loan sharking, gambling, and prostitution. If there was a crime in his jurisdiction, it came with his blessing and a tribute charge, and, it could be argued, if you wanted to be a state politician, you needed his blessing for that as well.

At his wake in 1984, strangers gathered outside with flowers to pay their respects. A reporter for the *Providence Journal* covering the wake quoted one bystander, who seemed to speak for the vast majority of onlookers: "I have more respect for this guy, and he never took an oath of office. Some of them who do get elected take an oath of office and steal the taxpayers blind."

It seems strange that my mother's path would cross with this man's, however peripherally. She was a nice Jewish girl from Cranston, and he was an old-fashioned gangster. They almost certainly never met in person. But in death, her name would be forever tied up with his—though his name is the one that people remember.

My mother's funeral didn't draw hundreds of admiring and curious onlookers. My mother was buried on a cold March day in a plot owned by my grandmother's employers, the Klitzner family. It had been intended for one of their own, which in a way my mom had been. It's one of the kindest and most practical gifts I can think of. Who would have expected that a thirty-year-old woman would need a burial plot?

———◆———

AT OUR MEETING, I ask Junior if he remembers my mom.

"See, this stuff now, it sickens me," he says. "I don't know. It's just I don't want to cry like a victim, but I have a lot of resentment toward my mom and dad. You know what I mean? Why wasn't I told to go to school? Why wasn't I taught to get a job and do all that good stuff that normal people do. As far as your mom goes, she was just another customer. She was a happy person. I don't know...Your mom? She was just an ideal woman. She had an addiction problem. It caused her death."

I want to say, no, that's wrong. It was your father that caused her death. It was him and Peter Gilbert that caused her death by murdering her. It was this culture of bravado and loyalty and getting over that killed her. But I don't say that because in a way, we are both right.

I ask him if he thinks there's any chance my mom actually was an informant, as his father believed.

"If your mother was the one that gave information about my father, then without a doubt it was because of her addiction," he says.

"She probably got pulled over and got caught with the drugs. They were going to arrest her. I can talk from that point of view because I've been addicted to heroin. I've been addicted to drugs for a long period of time, so I know. At that point in time, you just want to go home. You don't want to think about going to jail or being dope-sick or something like that. She would have gave the information to get out of there."

I'll never know if my mom gave confidential information to the police or not. I do know that almost everyone involved—from the men who killed her to the police who arrested them, to the attorney general who would strike a deal with Peter Gilbert—saw her as a disposable person. She was an addict. She prostituted herself for drugs. She sold other drugs to get cocaine. She was a means to an end.

SEVEN

———◆———

One night, soon after we move to Barrington, I feel stabbing pains in my right side during dinner.

"I don't feel good," I say. "Can I be excused?"

Dad and Ann-Marie roll their eyes at each across the table. It just so happens that we are eating beef stew that night, a dish I hate. The more I chew the chunks of stringy meat to get them down, the more flavorless they become until it feels like I'm gnawing away at gobs of tough leather.

"Finish your dinner," says Dad. He always shovels food into his mouth as fast as he can, as if someone is going to steal his plate away. Always suave in other circumstances, his eating habits are embarrassing. A lot of the time, he eats nothing all day and by dinner would be shoving food into his mouth, leaving a giant smear of sauce on his chin. Everything that goes down his throat is first filtered through the salt-and-pepper hairs of his mustache and sometimes hangs there, dangling, until he wipes it away with the back of his hand.

I take another bite of the stew and this time the pain in my side sharpens. It's like someone is jabbing a jagged broom handle into my right hip and then wiggling it around for good measure. I jump up from the table to vomit but don't make it to the bathroom in time. I hunch over, heaving beef stew all over the thick gray carpet in the living room.

"The toilet, Leah!" screams Ann-Marie, and so, still heaving, I toddle a few steps toward the bathroom dripping a trail of vomit behind me. "No, just stay!" Ann-Marie screams. "Just finish there!" And so I do, on my knees in front of the coffee table heaving and weeping as Dad holds my shoulder-length brown hair away from my face and rubs my back.

When I'm done and lying on the couch, Derek holds our dog Shilo back as Ann-Marie scrubs the carpet with an old rag. Dad stands over me, puts his hand against my forehead, and gives me a Kleenex to blow my nose. I hand him back the balled-up tissue when I'm done and say, "I told you I wasn't faking." I can still feel a pain in my side, duller now, and my head hurts from throwing up, but still it's satisfying to be proven right.

My mystery illness continues for weeks, and I miss more and more days of third grade. Some days I'll feel fine; sometimes I'll feel a pain like someone pinching and twisting my insides. Finally, after a third visit to the emergency room, Dad tells me I need to have surgery. He says the doctors don't know exactly what's wrong but that the surgery will fix it.

"You're a pretty sick kid but I promise to be there the whole time. I will never leave. I'll wait right outside the door the whole time." I hold on to Dad and breathe in his spicy, Polo scent. It makes me feel better to put my nose against his chest and inhale, knowing he'll be there to keep me safe, no matter what happens.

I can't eat anything for dinner that night, because I need an empty stomach for the surgery. Dad says the anesthesia will feel just like going to sleep and hours will go by, but it will feel like minutes and then the whole thing will be all over. And when I'm in the hospital I'll eat ice cream and Popsicles, and the best part will be that I won't feel so sick anymore. He makes up a bed for me on the couch and we sit together watching a movie of *Moby Dick* on television.

Dad explains that New Bedford, where the serial killer is, had been the whaling capital of the world in the days before electricity, when people used whale blubber to light their lamps at night. I fall asleep on the couch next to Dad after the white whale destroys Ahab's ship and Ishmael floats away on a coffin.

———◆———

THE NEXT MORNING in the hospital, two nurses come and lift me onto a gurney. Dad holds my hand as they wheel me into the hallway. "You'll be here when I wake up, right?"

"Of course." He has to stay on the other side of the swinging metal door as the orderlies push my gurney through.

They wheel me into the operating room. One of the nurses squeezes my hand and though she's wearing a surgical mask, I can tell by the way her eyes crinkle that she's smiling. "I feel weird," I tell her. The whole room seems far away and up close at the same time, like I'm watching what's going on from outside of myself, like the whole thing is on TV.

"That's just the medication," the nurse says. "You'll feel better soon." It seems like that is something people say a lot in the hospital. The same nurse holds a plastic mask next to my face and tells me that she's going to put it over my mouth. The doctor standing next to her says, "Now, the gas is going to smell funny, so what I want you to do is breathe it away from you, okay?"

"Okay." My heart pounds in my chest and the faraway feeling gets worse. I feel very trapped in the room, everything happening so fast, and the bright light above hurting my eyes. The nurse places the mask over my mouth and I jump. She holds my arm down and strokes my hand. From what feels like miles away I hear her say, "When I put this in your arm it's gonna feel icy," and then a slow coldness creeps into my fingers as she slides in the IV. "Okay, okaaaay, okaaaaaaaaaay," the nurse repeats, like a record in slow motion as I slip into unconsciousness.

After what feels like only a few moments, I wake with a start. All around my bed the faces of doctors and nurses stare down at me. I try to sit up and one of the nurses pushes me gently backward. I try to speak but my throat is parched and I seem to have forgotten how to make the words in my brain come out of my mouth. I'm crying.

"Ssshh," says the nurse. "It's okay, Leah. It's okay. You're waking up from surgery. We're going to give you this pain medicine and you'll feel better." She holds a syringe in her hand. I flail in my gurney, tugging at my IV. "I don't want a shot," I say, panicked. "I don't want a shot!"

"Leah." The nurse looks at me sternly. "After what you've been through, this shot is nothing. It's going to make you feel a lot better. I promise. And this"—she points at my IV—"if you pull this out they'll make me tie your arm down and I don't want to do that, okay?"

"I feel weird," I say.

"You're in the recovery room," says the nurse. "You're on a lot of medication. You just had a really big surgery."

"I want my dad," I say.

"Your mom is waiting for you in your room. You'll see her as soon as you're out of recovery."

I know she's talking about Ann-Marie. "She's not my mom."

"I'll keep an eye out," she says, looking intently at one of the machines by my gurney and making a note on my chart. "In the meantime you rest and feel better. We'll try to find your dad."

When they roll me into my hospital room from Recovery, Ann-Marie is waiting for me.

"Where's Dad?"

"He's on his way," she says. Her eyes are puffy and she's clutching a balled-up Kleenex.

"I want Dad," I whine, growing more desperate. The haze, the pain, I wasn't expecting any of it, and it seems like only Dad can make it better. "I'm so thirsty," I say. I have never been thirstier. I feel deep, dry cracks running along the insides of my mouth.

"Can she have some juice?" asks Ann-Marie.

"She can have some ice," says one of the nurses. "Just ice for right now."

Ann-Marie disappears into the hallway and comes back with a small plastic cup filled with shards of ice. She swirls the cup around and puts her hand on my forehead.

"I'm so thirsty," I say again. "I want juice."

"I'm sorry, Leah," she says. "The nurse says just ice right now." She holds the plastic cup to my mouth and gently shakes free a few chunks of ice. I suck at them, parched and desperate. In that moment, even as she takes care of me, after waiting hours for me to come out of surgery, I hate her. I hate that ice.

When I wake up next, Dad is sitting by my bed and Ann-Marie is gone.

"Hey kiddo," he says. His voice cracks and he starts to cry.

I've never seen my dad cry before. It makes no sense. But I'm so happy to see him I don't want to say anything that might make him leave again.

He looks smaller than normal from my angle on the bed. His mustache is droopy. His suit jacket hangs limply from the arm of his chair. The tears that fall from his eyes are long and slow.

"I love you," I tell him.

"I love you, too," he says. "Go back to sleep."

The next day, the doctors show me my scar—an eight-inch-long line held together with staples. The doctor says it's bigger than normal because they hadn't known exactly what they were looking for in there. What they found was a twisted fallopian tube. I've never heard the word before.

"Is that like my appendix?" In the weeks before, everyone had been telling me I might have appendicitis.

"It's a reproductive organ," he says, but doesn't explain anything else.

Dad keeps his word and is there every day. Together we poke at my hospital food. He pretends to steal bites of my Jell-O and I squeal in protest. He holds on to my saline drip as I hobble down the hallway, clutching the tender muscles of my sewn-up abdomen. He holds my hand as two nurses discover my head is covered in lice. They come to my hospital bed with a plastic washbasin filled with cold water, a metal hair pick, and an industrial-size bottle of shampoo.

"Please stop," I plead with them. "Please, please." The water is freezing and the metal picks sting my scalp.

"My goodness," says a nurse to my dad. "I've never

seen so much thick hair!" She looks at the metal comb, holds it up to the fluorescent light. "Or, to be honest, so many lice. They like clean hair, you know. No need to be embarrassed."

Dad smiles at her and tips his tall body back in the chair. "Well, Leah is attached to her little pets."

The nurse giggles, shakes her head, and dips the metal comb into a bowl of soap and water. Dad has amassed a small fan club of nurses who slip us extra rice pudding and are always popping in just to say hi. They all love Dad. The nurse from the recovery room comes by to check on the little girl who asked only for her dad and not her mom.

Dad sits next to my hospital bed and reads me a book called *The Enormous Egg*, about a boy in New Hampshire who hatches a dinosaur egg on his farm. At every chapter break Dad tells me I have to get up and move around or I will have to stay in the hospital longer. We walk slowly up and down the green-and-white hallways of the hospital, and the next chapter of the book is my reward for the effort.

One morning, a man in an enormous Alf costume walks into my room carrying a bouquet of balloons. I creep as far back into my bed as I can, afraid to look at the horrifying character.

"Hellooooo!" Alf says, his snout looming over me. "I heard you were a very sick lady so I brought you some balloons!"

I reach silently for the balloons.

"Shake my hand?" asks Alf.

I feel terrible being so rude, but there is just no way I can do it. He holds out his tan furry paw and it comes at me in slow motion. "No," I say, then in rapid succession as I begin to panic, "no no no no no."

Alf chuckles. "Enjoy your balloons," he says and waddles out of the room. I hear him as he makes his way down the halls, saying hello to the other sick children: the boy with whooping cough who hacks all day long, the girl with asthma so bad she sleeps inside a tent, the baby twins with some kind of rash. I wonder if they are all as freaked out as I am.

"Dad?" I ask.

"I think the guys from work thought it would be nice," he says. "Six-foot Alf is not too cool when you're high on morphine?"

"Can we finish the book?" I ask.

IN JUNE 1988, around the same time I am having surgery for my twisted fallopian tube, Peter Gilbert, one of the two men who'd murdered my mom, is headed down Connecticut Route 101 on his way to go skydiving. As he suddenly stops short, the man in the car behind him hits his brakes, curses at Gilbert, and drives away. Gilbert follows, infuriated, pushing both cars to ninety miles an hour before they pull off into a gas station parking lot. Gilbert gets out of his car brandishing a lead-filled blackjack, while an off-duty

Connecticut State Police trooper who happens to be at the scene rushes to break up the fight. He arrests Gilbert and asks his permission to search the car, which comes back as registered to the Providence police. Gilbert, sweating and shaking, opens the trunk, pops a pill, and falls to the ground. He's pronounced dead, at age forty-four, of a massive heart attack when he arrives at a nearby hospital.

In his trunk is a parachute bag and nineteen packets of cocaine.

So how did Peter Gilbert wind up dead, alone, with a weapon and drugs and a vehicle belonging to the police?

In February 1985, four months after he and Gerald Mastracchio Sr. murdered my mom, Gilbert's home was raided by the Providence police and he was taken into custody for possession of drug paraphernalia and illegal weapons. He was hopelessly hooked on cocaine at this point, having his wife inject him every morning and walking around wearing a tourniquet so that when it was time to shoot up, he wouldn't have to waste a moment. When the police brought him in he was five foot five and weighed just 110 pounds.

He'd recently committed three murders. First, my mom. Then another man named Joe West, whom Gilbert shot in the head as West sat in his car under an overpass. With the help of Gerald Mastracchio Jr. he'd killed a man named Joe Olivo who, like my mother, was suspected of being an informant. They strangled him with a necktie but it broke. They shot him but he continued to gurgle. After a second shot, he died. Later, Gilbert helped saw Joe Olivo into pieces, pour acid over tattoos that might identify him, and toss his body parts into various dumpsters around the state.

An independent investigation into how his protective custody had gone so awry would later conclude, "Given the nature of his crimes...it appears Gilbert received far greater benefits from his bargain than did the State of Rhode Island."

GILBERT WAS ARRESTED that morning in February at nine o'clock. By eleven that night he'd confessed to armed robbery, murder, and being the second in command of a wholesale drug operation: All of these crimes, he promised, were overseen by the Patriarca family. He was fearful for his life, he told the police, and for the lives of his family. In exchange for testimony, he wanted protection. When he was done detailing his crimes, he and his arresting officers, Detective Oates and Lieutenant Tamburini, settled in for a "nice Italian meal" they ordered and ate at the Providence police station.

The next morning the attorney general's office met with Gilbert. After agreeing that everything he said was credible they struck a deal. The murder 1 charges (premeditated) would be struck down to murder 2, and he wouldn't be charged in the armed robbery or the drug conspiracy. In exchange for his testimony, his sentence for the murder charges would be ten years, to be served in the protection of the Providence police. He would also have outstanding warrants for his arrest in Florida and Maine eliminated.

He'd stay right where he was in Rhode Island. In return for his information that he swore would take down the mob, the state would foot the bill for all of his living expenses. The Providence police had no experience in witness protection or relocation. There was no plan for what they'd do with such a seemingly valuable asset. Somehow, someone, somewhere, made the decision to start construction right there in the station to build Gilbert a proper apartment where they could keep him safe. He had a small kitchen, a living room, and a bedroom. He kept a pet bird and a poodle named Cuddles. His wife and young children were allowed to stay with him and at night, they "played court" in the courtroom downstairs.

The state of Rhode Island and the Providence Police Department did whatever they thought would keep their star witness as happy as possible. And Gilbert took full advantage of the benefits he discovered he could extract as that star witness: free take-out meals, trips to Florida, a vacation home in Narragansett over Christmas with his family, and welfare checks for him and his wife. With no clear leadership, and no established set of practices, it was easy for a con artist like Gilbert to dangle his supposed connections to the mafia and demand more and more.

He needed to exercise, of course, so he got some roller skates and skated through the halls of the police building. He needed transportation so he was given access to the vehicles belonging to the Providence Police Department; after he died and the state and journalists went through the receipts, they found he'd purchased, with the state's money and help, a motorcycle, shoeshines, trips to the bowling alley, ammunition, throwing stars, and, of course, the skydiving lessons.

The longer he was around, the more he got to know some of the cops. Maybe he felt like he was a kind of cop. Certainly many of the officers, seeing him day in and day out, treated him like a friend if not a colleague. Gilbert may have actually begun to believe he was doing a great civic duty and that he should be rewarded for it, over and over again. And for nearly four years, the state of Rhode Island continued to reward him beyond any scope of what a protected witness was entitled to, until he died, on his way to skydive. Free fall must have seemed like the ultimate freedom.

Shortly after his death, the RICO indictment was vacated. Raymond Patriarca hadn't even lived to see it filed. He died of a heart attack in 1984 and his incompetent son, his namesake, Raymond Patriarca Jr., allegedly took over the business. Nobody trusted him like they had his father.

———◆———

WHEN GILBERT DIED, his strange deal was made public. It was a huge scandal; the evidence of such gross corruption and incompetence was shocking, even by Rhode Island standards.

There was an independent investigation into the matter but in the end, the attorney general's office pointed the finger at the Providence police and the Providence police said they were just doing what the attorney general told them to do and the mayor said he didn't even have any knowledge of this deal, and nothing, not one single good thing, not a single shred of anything gallant or fair came out of any of it. And when, two decades later, I called Lieutenant Tamburini, one of the officers who'd been in charge of Gilbert's custody and testimony, and explained to him who my mom was and that I was looking for information about the details surrounding her murder, he told me, "I don't really understand what any of this has to do with you. That was a very difficult time in my life and I don't think I'll be talking to you about it." He's now the chief of police in a town neighboring Providence.

They hadn't cared about my mom then and they don't care about her now.

———

THE *PROVIDENCE JOURNAL*, particularly a young reporter named Dean Starkman, wrote many comprehensive articles about Gilbert, the Patriarca crime family, and the drug trade in Rhode Island. Starkman came the closest to explaining how something like this could have happened when he wrote, "Gilbert's testimony shines a harsh light on a layer of the underworld rarely seen by outsiders. It's not the organized crime of high-ranking mobsters in limousines and $1,000 suits. And it's nothing like the romantic popular mystique of the Mafia as a well-organized brotherhood of 'men of honor.' Gilbert's world is a kingdom of ugliness, where men without conscience rule over drug users, enslaved both by their addiction and by their rulers' breathtaking capacity for violence."

———•———

FOR ME, IN all the piles of information that exist about the Gilbert affair, there is one small detail that stands out in particular. Among the many receipts is one for an electric typewriter. Gilbert was writing his memoirs while in "protective custody." He was sure they'd be optioned for a movie. He wrote, "I gave the police my statements involving myself in three murders and a robbery...and having to do a few years wasn't a bad deal."

But Peter Gilbert doesn't get to tell this story.

I do.

EIGHT

— ◆ —

I spend the summer after fifth grade lounging, mostly, in front of the television in the living room, and in my un-air-conditioned room. I'm so afraid of kidnappers and murderers that I don't dare leave the window open while I sleep and I wake at night, sweating in the stifling heat.

We have a patio that Ann-Marie and Dad built themselves by filling a wide wooden frame with concrete and flagstones. In the summer Dad puts on mesh shorts and tans out there in a lounge chair. His face is already pink, and crisscrossed with tiny delicate purple veins on his cheeks and at the edges of his eyes and nose. As the summer goes on he grows redder and redder until, from a distance, his bright-red face and silver hair are almost shocking as he walks toward you.

Our dead end street is perfectly still most days, filled only with the sounds of cicadas and, in the distance, children's soccer games being played at the middle school. Overhead, very dimly, you can hear the low rumble of the airplane engines as they fly over us on their way from or back to T. F. Green Airport in Warwick.

Dad always has a stack of books next to him, and he balances a glass of ice cubes and water on top. He moves among Tom Clancy thrillers, books on photography, and biographies of ex-presidents. That summer I read *Clan of the Cave Bear*, and work my way through most of the V. C. Andrews books, all checked out from our local library. I love the dirty sections and am proud that I'm allowed to read whatever I want. I think the prose is dark and gothic and wonderful and spend many nights in my sweltering bedroom writing my own stories of intrigue and death. The main character is usually what I imagine myself to be in ten years. I describe her as "no-nonsense" with "raven-colored" hair.

Dad's hours at the *Journal* are erratic, and while most days Derek and I have the house to ourselves, we share many with Dad, lying on the porch, reading. The beach in Newport is about thirty minutes away, but we rarely go. Sometimes we drive down to the little slip of sand that is Barrington Beach to take photos of the sunset. There Dad teaches me to count out the seconds before pressing the button connected to a cord that closes the camera shutter remotely. This way you don't shake the lens. No matter how still you think you're standing, the camera will always shake if you don't use a tripod.

On the Fourth of July, we set up Dad's camera on the seawall to take pictures of the fireworks across the bay in Newport. The air smells like barbecue and seaweed. Dad shows me the exact moment to snap the pictures and when we get them developed, the fireworks on film seem far more spectacular than the ones I'd witnessed with my own eyes.

———•———

EARLY IN THE school year, Ann-Marie takes me to the dentist for a cleaning. Cleanings are traumatic, because I never, ever escape without at least one filling. Dad says I have soft teeth, like him. He had two teeth pulled in Vietnam and when he smiles wide you can just see the gap where they should have been. He says that was the first time he'd been to the dentist in his whole life. All his front teeth are capped and sometimes a cap falls off, revealing the gray stump of old tooth. Dad is vain, constantly preening in the mirror and fluffing his silver hair, but when a cap falls out he flashes his jack-o'-lantern grin for days, thrilled by my shrieks of horror.

We sit in the dentist's office, lite rock playing softly from the speakers above us. I hope some disaster might happen that will keep me from the dentist's office: from his drill, and latex gloves, and Novocain shots. Maybe the roof will cave in, or outside the office, on Route 195, a car will careen past the Jersey barriers into the Barrington River. Then all these thoughts of sealants, fillings, and fluoride trays will be forgotten as we rush outside to survey the damage.

Flipping through the *People* in the dentist's office, I come across an article about the recent invasion of Kuwait that describes Kuwaitis fleeing the border there, racing desperately across the desert to escape an evil dictator named Saddam Hussein. In one story a family traveling by car stopped to give a man on foot the only beverage they could spare: a warm can of Diet Coke. I think of how terrible that must be, the warm, tinny, chemical taste in the middle of the blazing desert. The article describes Kuwait, a tiny country near the base of Saudi Arabia, as being "roughly the size of Rhode Island."

"Look!" I show Ann-Marie. "This article is talking about Rhode Island!"

She looks at the paragraph. "They only talk about Rhode Island when they want to describe something small. Something big is the size of Texas. Something small is the size of Rhode Island." I feel like our state is famous and read on with intense interest, wondering why a dictator would even bother to invade a country so small. Finally the hygienist opens the door and calls my name. She's all smiles as I reluctantly put down the magazine and follow her back to the dentist's chair.

I'm fascinated by the Gulf War and watch the constant coverage on CNN. During the slow buildup to the fighting the news anchors sometimes run out of things to talk about and walk around on a huge map of the Middle East pointing at Kuwait, Iraq, and Saudi Arabia. Sometimes they hold up gas masks and demonstrate how the soldiers will need to use them if Saddam decides to gas the troops. They talk about all the terrible things Saddam has done to his people, the size of his army, and the scorching temperatures in the desert.

I imagine that this was what it had been like in the 1960s when Dad went to Vietnam. He was only seventeen when he enlisted, and while seventeen seems grown-up to my eleven-year-old mind, I understand how young it is to go to war. In class we write letters to the soldiers and I pour my heart out to them, telling them how brave they are, and how much their sacrifice matters to the country.

One afternoon as Derek and I watch TV, Lee Greenwood sings "Proud to Be an American" at a sporting event. My heart swells as his voice rises with the chorus and F-14 fighter jets fly overhead, leaving behind a red, white, and blue vapor trail. Dad comes out of the bedroom and stands in the doorway between the living room and the kitchen looking at the TV. "Now, that's some bullshit," he says. I'm embarrassed; the pride that had filled me leaves my body in a breath. "What do you mean?"

"It's just fake, patriotic, NASCAR-loving bullshit," he says. "When I left Vietnam I threw my medals at the White House. They meant nothing. The government is using those kids up."

"So you were a hippie, then?" I sit up from where I'd been lounging on my side of the couch with my head in my left hand, my right hand holding a book open—my usual position. I pick at the tan and red tweed fibers of the couch. On the TV, the song is over and and the game has started. Sunlight pours in through the window on my left and cuts a long rectangle across the group of houseplants Ann-Marie keeps there. There are layers of dust on the leaves.

"I wasn't a hippie, Leah. I was a poor kid from South Providence. That's why I went to Vietnam in the first place. What else was I going to do?"

"But you thought the war was bad?" It's hard to wrap my mind around Dad's answers. I had thought you were either a hippie in the 1960s, or you were a veteran. I don't understand how being poor has anything to do with anything.

"War is fucked, kiddo," said Dad. "But it's the best people in our country who fight them. And the ones who don't have any other choice." Walking into the kitchen he says over his shoulder, "And that song sucks. Since when does my daughter listen to country music?"

"I don't!" I call back.

Dad's attitude toward the wars—the Gulf War and the Vietnam War—continue to confuse me. At Aunty Rita's house, we watch the footage of a Patriot missile blowing a SCUD missile out of the sky and everyone cheers. But Dad's more concerned with the politics of it all—what are the president's real motives; is this about oil, religion?

One night I walk into our living room, after the fighting has officially begun, and Dad watches TV in the dark. On screen, oil fires rage against the black sky.

"Now, that's something," he says.

It all ends so fast, the occupation, the war, it is like I never have time to fully take it in. But I have such a funny feeling watching the troops on TV. I think they looked scared and sad, and wonder if that's how Dad had felt, and if he sometimes feels that way now.

———⋅———

THAT FALL I sit at the kitchen table as Ann-Marie cooks dinner, and I read an article in the *Providence Journal* about a missing family from Barrington, the Brendels.

"What do you think happened to them?" I ask.

"Who knows?" Ann-Marie opens a bag of macaroni and pours it into the stockpot. "I hope nothing bad. That poor little girl. So weird."

The missing Brendel family are a father, a mother, and an eight-year-old girl, Emily, who is in the third grade. The picture of them from the paper looks strangely dated, like a family from decades before my time. The mom has a bowl-shaped haircut. I think she looks like a Pilgrim, and very different from Ann-Marie, who is stylish and gets her clothes at the Cherry & Webb store. I think the dad is old looking to have such a young daughter. And the photo itself is taken in a portrait studio—something we never do as a family. We don't even buy school photos, since Dad takes better, cooler pictures anyway. (Though when the pictures come back I pine for my own stack of wallet-size photos that everyone else trades like baseball cards.)

"When they say foul play," I say, looking over the article, "they mean murder, right?"

"Well, I don't know about that!" says Ann-Marie. "This is Barrington. Whole families don't just get murdered." She dumps the egg noodles into a large glass bowl, then pours in peas and steak tips, mixing it all together. My stomach churns at the sight.

"So you think they just left the house and went somewhere?"

This makes a kind of sense to me. Next to our house is a lot filled with briar bushes, vines, and a massive pit, on top of which there had once been a ramshackle house. The family that lived in the house took off one day and abandoned everything. I had heard Fran from across the street tell Ann-Marie that they'd left their dog in the closet, and by the time anyone had gone into the house, the dog was dead. Soon after the city bulldozed the house, but nobody has yet bought the land, and so the lot fills with more weeds and the pit slowly caves in on itself. I think about the dog a lot and try to never look at where the house had been.

Maybe the Brendels have done something like that, I wonder. I know the family next door had been behind on their mortgage, according to Fran. Ann-Marie is right. Barrington is a safe place. It's not the kind of place where you get kidnapped or murdered. The adults, all of our parents and teachers, talk about the case nonstop, and as sixth graders we pick up on what they say and whisper it among ourselves.

———•———

IN BARRINGTON, WE pride ourselves on being the wealthiest town in Rhode Island. It's a town where almost nobody speaks in the thick Rhode Island accent of my grandparents and my aunts. It's a town of lawyers and doctors and the wives and children of lawyers and doctors. It's a place where you buy a boat, a Volvo, and a golden retriever. It isn't the kind of place where people get murdered, especially not an eight-year-old girl, her librarian mother, and her lawyer father. Especially not a family who lives in a quaint little carriage house on the corner of Middle Road, which, if maybe not the most exclusive neighborhood in Barrington, is certainly nice.

If my family doesn't fit that mold, if my dad isn't a lawyer, but instead is in charge of the trucks at the *Providence Journal*, if he drives a Mitsubishi with tinted windows and blasts WBRU, the local alternative radio station, and if he calls Bryan Adams a hack when his song that everyone loves from the movie *Robin Hood* comes on, and instead turns up the Red Hot Chili Peppers, that's fine. That's what makes us special and different and cool. But we're surrounded by things that are normal and wealthy and safe. Which means we, in turn, are safe.

Maybe, I sometimes think, if we had always lived in

Barrington, Mom would never have been murdered. Maybe if Dad had grown up in Barrington and not in the triple-decker house on Eddy Street in South Providence, then his mom would not have drunk herself to an early death, his dad would not have hated him, he would never have gone to Vietnam, and he wouldn't be an alcoholic now. Maybe if I stay in Barrington long enough, if we are a family in Barrington long enough, all that safe wealthy stuff—the skiing, the Volvos, the trips to Martha's Vineyard, and the sailboating in Narragansett Bay—will work their way into our genes and we'll become, if not normal, then at the very least, safe.

———◆———

FIRST, THE POLICE find teeth and blood in the Brendel garage. And then, near the middle of November, they find the bodies.

We're in social studies, where recently Mrs. Robbins has called me "little Murphy Brown" for a journalism project I worked on, and another girl in class rolled her eyes and said that I was Mrs. Robbins's pet even though I never did my homework and therefore had cost the class a pizza party. The intercom over the door crackles to life and our principal comes on the speaker.

"Attention students, attention students," he clears his throat. "After-school activities are cancelled for the day. Bussers, please report immediately to bus pickup after school. Walkers, please report to the principal's office after school."

When the intercom turns off, the class buzzes with excitement.

"They found the Brendels!" says Brett, one of the popular boys. He has sandy-colored hair and braces and wears Umbro shorts with his boxers hanging out the bottom hem.

"Brett!" Mrs. Robbins chides. "Don't say that." She picks up the coffee mug on her desk and takes a big sip of water. A drop trickles onto her chin and when she wipes it off she smears her lipstick a tiny bit. In her teacher clothes and frizzy hair, the pink smudge on her chin makes her look ever-so-slightly crazy.

When school is over for the day, I bypass the principal's office. I am a walker—we live too close to the school to be picked up by the bus. I know that Ann-Marie won't be home from work yet and that if Dad is home, he's probably asleep. I walk out the door for bussers and then creep around the back of the school building to cut across the baseball field and running track and take my usual route home. When I get home, I turn on the TV in the living room and curl up on the couch with Shilo at my feet. I close my eyes to take a nap, something I often do after school, and something Ann-Marie thinks is strange.

"Kids her age aren't supposed to take naps," she has told Dad. "What's making her so tired?" But I am tired, almost all the time, and particularly after school. It's the kind of bone-weariness that makes it almost painful to keep my eyes open. When I explain this to my pediatrician, she sends me in for a bunch of tests that all come back negative. No anemia, no vitamin deficiency, no narcolepsy. The pediatrician says to Ann-Marie, "Some people just need more sleep than other people." There's no reason. I'm not sick. I'm just always tired.

I wake to the sound of Derek crashing through the door, knocking coats off the coatrack with his overstuffed backpack.

"I think they found the Brendels," I tell him.

"I know," he says. "There are all these police cars down by St. Andrew's field."

Our street, Carpenter Avenue, is a dead end that turns into St. Andrew's field, a small meadow with an abandoned barn and a patch of woods. I often take Shilo for walks in the field, acting out imaginary scenarios in which I'm on a romantic stroll with Brett, or eluding a teenage murderer who is obsessed with my beauty and intelligence.

This is what we learn from the *Journal* and the TV news: Though the police had been searching for the bodies for nearly a month, it was a woman walking her dog who actually finds them. The dad had been buried in one grave and had crossbow wounds to the chest. The mother and daughter were in another shallow grave together across the street from St. Andrew's field. The mom had been strangled, but the police can't find a cause of death for little Emily.

The murderer is a local man, a man with a wife and young son of his own. His name is Christopher Hightower, and he lives in a big house on Nayatt Avenue near the water. Hightower himself had picked little Emily up from the after-school program at the YMCA (the same one I'd gone to). He'd once been a family friend and she'd gone with him willingly. I wonder what would have happened if Christopher Hightower had seen me in the field sometime by myself. Would he have hurt me? Would he have hurt Shilo if she tried to protect me?

———◆———

AT THANKSGIVING, AT Ann-Marie's parents' house, her four brothers and their wives rest after the meal in the living room, sprawled out on the brocade sofas. Most of the grandchildren play in the basement, but I stay upstairs and stick close to Dad. It's in a setting like this that he is often at his best, and I love to watch him. He can argue any political fact, cite any arcane literary reference, and the brothers all love him. They laugh at his jokes, slapping their knees, and nod deeply at points well made, creasing their chins and agreeing, "Okay, okay, I can see what you're saying."

But this Thanksgiving everyone talks about the Brendels.

"It's just gruesome," says Grandma Anne. "I still can't believe it happened. And the little girl!" She clucks and shakes her head.

"Well, did you hear they think he buried her alive?" somebody volunteers. "Gave her a ton of cough syrup and then just threw her in the grave with the mom on top of her. They're saying she smothered to death."

This seems so horrible that I instantly picture it in my

head, the darkness and dirt. I hope it's not true. I hope that at least she'd been strangled before being buried. Dad is silent throughout the conversation. He sits in one of Grandma Anne's wingback chairs reading a *Smithsonian* magazine. I look for something in his face, but it's blank.

———·———

ONE NIGHT, DEREK and I are at the kitchen table playing Uno, when we hear the particular sounds of Dad's very drunk footsteps coming across the patio to the side door. Dad fumbles a bit with the door while we sit there, and when he comes in, everything seems okay at first. He's in a suit, upright but a bit wobbly. Then he turns to face us. The entire right side of his head is soaked in blood. It drips from his hair and onto his shoulders. His eye is swollen shut. He stands and looks at us as if daring us to look away. Neither of us do. Then he walks through the kitchen and makes his way to the bedroom. He leaves behind a trail of penny-size drops of blood.

Just as Ann-Marie comes running into the kitchen, our house lights up in flashes of blue and white and there's a heavy knock at the door. Outside are half a dozen police officers. Their cars are parked on the street and in our yard and the officers stand solemnly in bright-yellow slickers to protect themselves from the drizzle that has turned to rain. The entire front end of Dad's car is mangled, into an almost symmetrical U shape. The windshield is bloody but not smashed. Instead there's a bubble in the glass—an imprint that Dad's head must have made as it slammed forward.

Ann-Marie talks to the officers and I grab a kitchen sponge to clean up the splotches of blood. When I squeeze the sponge into the kitchen sink I look out the window and see the neighbors peering at our house from between their blinds and half-open doors.

Ann-Marie is hysterical. Derek has fled to his room. But I'm angry. I'm angry at the gawkers across the street and all the stupid flashing police cars. One of the officers tells Ann-Marie that if she doesn't get Dad to come out of the house on his own, they will have to come inside and get him. I stand in the bedroom door as she tries to rouse him from sleep, the bloody half of his face slowly turning his pillow red. Eventually, the police come in and haul him to his feet. "Okay, okay," he says to them. "Okay, okay."

I'm blocking the narrow hallway that leads from the bedroom to the kitchen and one of the cops tells me to get out of the way. It surprises me actually, how angry the officer seems at me. In the kitchen two officers prop Dad up on either side and walk him out the door. Ann-Marie weeps silently next to me. I still have the bloody sponge in my hand. Dad turns to look at us with his monster face. "Thanks a lot, you fucking bitches," he says so clearly it echoes through the dark house, lit up only by the flashing blue and white of the police cruisers.

When he gets back the next morning, Dad has a big bandage covering his right eye and goes right to sleep.

Derek and I listen as he and Ann-Marie murmur behind the closed bedroom door. His car, which he had wrapped around a telephone pole at the bottom of the street and then somehow extracted and driven home, has been towed away. Later, we sit in the living room and Dad tells us he's going to the VA hospital for a few weeks. He says he's going for alcohol detox and to get electroshock therapy for his depression. It all sounds bleak and terrifying to me, but Dad seems excited.

"Everything will be better after this," he says.

"Do you have to go to jail?" I ask. Dad rolls his eyes at me. Why *am* I such a bitch, I wonder.

———•———

WHEN HE GETS back from the VA hospital, he has a new diagnosis: manic depression. This is why he sleeps so much and disappears for days. He can't drink now, because he's on a drug called Antabuse that makes him really sick if he does. For years now, Dad hasn't had a drink in front of us. We don't keep alcohol in the house, though once poking around in the basement, I'd opened a case for one of his big telephoto lenses and found a half-empty bottle of Jameson's inside.

But now he's on a cocktail of new medications and some of them make him seem drunk. He shows us his prescriptions lined up on the windowsill above the kitchen sink looking out onto Carpenter Avenue. He shakes the brown prescription bottles, rattling the pills inside, and explains, "These are Klonopin, these are Xanax, this is lithium, this is Prozac. All of these are prescribed for a big two-hundred-pound guy, and if you or Derek tried to take one to see what it was like, you could die."

I have no interest in taking Dad's pills, but I watch his consumption of them closely. That summer he takes me and a friend to see *Batman Returns* at the Showcase Cinemas in Seekonk and lingers behind us in the car, shaking a pill from the bottle and swallowing it dry. He jumps triumphantly out of the car and squeezes my shoulders, shaking me back and forth. "Ready?" he asks. "This one won't be as good as the last one because there's no Joker in this one." Then he does his imitation of Jack Nicholson dancing to the Prince song all the way up to the doors of the theater. My friend giggles.

During the movie, Dad gets up to go to the bathroom twice and takes another pill in the theater. He's right. The sequel is not as good as the first Batman movie. As we walk back to the car he staggers a bit. From the front seat of the car he does his Joker impression again, but this time it's in slow motion. I watch the road as we pull onto the Wampanoag Trail, the short freeway that connects Barrington to Seekonk and Providence. Dad swerves to his left and nearly swipes a mini van at one point. I seem to be the only one who notices. Dad turns up the music on the car radio and sings along and my friend laughs in the backseat and puffs on her inhaler. She always has a brown paper bag with at least two inhalers for her chronic asthma, and normally I would be both jealous of her affliction and annoyed by the puffing and the attention it gets her, but I'm too busy keeping track of Dad's driving. I pretend to listen intently to the radio, all the while aware of Dad's physical presence in the car, and monitor how close he is to me, where he's looking, or if he's looking at all.

PART TWO

NINE

One day in May of 1993, a few months before I turn thirteen, Dad says to me, "Ann-Marie is having a baby." It isn't totally unexpected. Months before, Ann-Marie had purchased a home fertility test, and for a while there were a bunch of negative pregnancy test sticks in the bathroom trash, but then we'd heard nothing else about having a baby. I'm excited by the idea of a baby. I think a baby might be able to fix our family.

We aren't allowed to tell anyone for another month— until after Ann-Marie has passed her first trimester. It's possible, she tells us, that she can lose the baby during that time so it's better to wait. I'm anxious every day, counting down on my wall calendar, terrified to say anything lest I jinx the pregnancy and make Ann-Marie have a miscarriage. Finally, in June, she says it's safe.

I call Aunty Sandy, and tell her the news. "Oh," she says.

"Isn't it exciting?" I ask.

"Mm-hm."

Aunty Sandy is married now with a little girl, but she lives just down the street from my grandparents. Her response makes my stomach sink, and I'm worried my grandma will also act like it's bad news. I don't want to press Sandy on her real feelings because I'm worried she'll say something I don't want to hear. The summer is coming and seventh grade is ending and I am going to have a real family with a baby. I decide that if I can be happy enough about it then it will all work out perfectly. I'll prove to my grandparents and to Aunty Sandy that I can make everything okay.

———•———

TAYLOR IS BORN in December. Ann-Marie's water breaks in the middle of the night a few days after Christmas and she and Dad grab the overnight bag she packed a few days before and take off for Women & Infants Hospital in Providence. I pace around the house and go to the basement to try to get Derek to stay up with me.

"Just wake me up when the baby's born." He pulls a pillow over his head.

I turn the TV off and on and think about calling someone but it's too late at night. Dad comes back home just as the sun is rising. From my room I hear him come inside and when I walk into the kitchen he's talking on the cordless phone sitting at the table. He has on sweatpants and shiny leather loafers and I can smell alcohol on him. He looks up at me but continues his conversation.

"Well," he says into the phone. "Taylor's here. The umbilical cord was wrapped around her neck so they had to give Ann-Marie an emergency C-section but everything's okay now."

My eyes widen and Dad winks at me. "Yup," he says. I can tell he's trying to wind down the conversation and guess that he's talking to Ann-Marie's parents. "We'll see you in the morning," he says clicking the OFF button of the phone and putting it down between us on the table.

"She's okay?" I ask.

"They are both okay," says Dad. His words are thick, not slurred, but slow and laden with a kind of sadness that I hear only when he has been drinking whiskey and not beer. "Taylor is a little peanut. You're going to love her." He stops for a moment and looks out the window at the dull gray sky of the early winter morning. There's something in his mustache, a brown spot, maybe gravy or ketchup, and I stare hard at it. This is not what I'd hoped for. Dad wasn't supposed to come home drunk with food in his mustache. I wonder if Ann-Marie and Taylor are sleeping or awake in the hospital and wondering where Dad was.

"When can we go see her?"

"Visiting hours start soon," he says. "You're going to love her. I know you will."

"Of course I will," I say, my voice unintentionally sharp. Of course I will love my baby sister. I'm a normal person. Dad looks at me, surprised. Though I talk back to all my teachers and pride myself on my smart mouth, I almost never take a tone with Dad, especially if he has been drinking.

"You know when you were born," he says, "I was in a fucking locked room in the hospital basement." He laughs. "I guess I've come a long way, huh?"

I smile at him, despite myself. "You have food on your face," I tell him. He laughs again and scratches at his mustache with his thumb and forefinger, dislodging what's crusted there.

His eyes are bloodshot and tiny red veins creep across his nose and the top of his cheeks where they met his crinkled eyelids. He holds his hand out and I grab it across the table. He squeezes and tells me the story of when I was born and though I've heard it before, I listen, because it's a good story and because I know Dad likes telling it.

My mother's doctor, it turns out, was a raging alcoholic, and when my mom went into labor with me, he'd been on a bender for days and the nurses, who were terrified of him, tried to buy some time to sober him up and kept coming up with excuses for why they couldn't call him. My family, unaware of the doctor's state, grew increasingly agitated as the hours went by. I was a big baby, almost eight pounds, and my mom was a tiny lady, not just short but built with the same kind of small bones as me.

"And so your mom is in labor for nine, ten, eleven hours," Dad says. "And the nurses won't call the doctor and your grandmother is freaking out and I'm yelling for someone to help her out. And then finally they send in this security guard, this fucking rent-a-cop, who's telling me 'calm down, calm down' and he's about five foot five and I pick up the chair I'm sitting in and wing it across the room and ask him if I'm calm enough and the next thing there are nine guys wrestling me down and your grandma is screaming and your mom, at this point, probably doesn't even notice, and then I'm in a locked room when you're finally born. And my God, you were an ugly baby!" Dad says that by the time the doctor finally came, it was too late for a C-section and they had to pull me out with high forceps and I was covered in bruises, jaundiced, and had a malformed head.

"But you got better," says Dad. "Wait till you see her. She's a little peanut." He swallows the rest of his glass and kicks off his loafers. "We'll go in a few hours," he says. "Just wake me up in a few hours." He walks out of the kitchen, headed for his bedroom, leaving a trail of clothes in his wake.

I DO, OF course, love Taylor. Even during the first few months when she does little more than ball her hands into tiny fists and scream, I'm captivated. I hold her in the gliding chair in her nursery and watch as she squeezes her eyes open and closed and tenses all her muscles. I listen carefully as Ann-Marie explains how to change her diaper, how to wipe the folds of her chubby thighs so she doesn't get a rash, how to walk her around bopping up and down and patting rhythmically at her back until she burps or throws up all over the cloth Ann-Marie places on my shoulder.

From the start, Taylor is more mine than Dad's. After her three months of maternity leave are over, Ann-Marie reluctantly goes back to work and Taylor goes to daycare. The first week, Dad says he'll take care of getting the baby ready and driving her to daycare, because he's working nights at the *Journal*. When I go with Ann-Marie that first afternoon to pick Taylor up, Denise, the babysitter, hands over Taylor and her heavily packed diaper bag.

"Men!" she says and laughs nervously. Dad had dropped Taylor off that morning with poop all over her stomach and legs. He'd seemingly put a new diaper on her but had not bothered to clean any of the mess from the old one before snapping her clothes together. Denise tries to act like Dad is just a typical sitcom male, unaware of how to change a diaper, but we all know better. That same week I'd asked Dad if he could drive Derek and me to school. Ann-Marie had left for work and he sat in the living room, Taylor asleep at his feet in her bassinet.

"I guess so," he said, and walked to the hook in the kitchen where he hung his car keys. I reached for the sleeping baby, ready to carry her out and buckle her into the car seat myself.

"Just leave her," said Dad. "That whole thing with the car seat will take too long."

My heart seized up in my chest and beside me Derek stiffened.

"We'll just walk then," I said.

"I said she'll be fine," Dad said. His look was menacing as he loomed over us. "Do you think I've never done this before?"

Derek and I trudged out to the car, with Taylor asleep on the living room floor. As Dad dropped us off and Derek and I walked through the front doors, Derek turned to me and said, "That was really fucked up, right? Like that's normally not what you do with a baby, right?"

"Don't tell Ann-Marie," I said. Derek shrugged.

"Seriously," I said. "You can't tell her."

———————

THAT APRIL, WHEN I'm in eighth grade and Taylor learns how to crawl around the house, Kurt Cobain kills himself. I watch the coverage on MTV obsessively—the footage of his Converse-clad feet seen from the window of the tiny shed in which he'd shot himself, the interviews with friends, acquaintances, and experts who opine about what this means for music, the memorial service in Seattle where Courtney Love reads from sections of his suicide note, her voice cracking with grief over the loudspeakers as she speaks of the "burning, nauseous, pit" inside Kurt's stomach.

I collect all the magazines I can get my hands on: *Spin*, *Rolling Stone*, even *People*, and pore over the articles trying to figure out how it could have happened. Everyone talks about how young he was. I can't get over the pictures of his young daughter with her bright blue eyes, so much like Kurt's. And the nature of it—shooting yourself in the head with a shotgun. I understand that a person only does that when they truly want out, truly don't want to live anymore. I think there's something courageous about it—the finality.

That year my best friend and I think we're the only ones in school who really understand Kurt Cobain and his music. I spend hours in the TV room of her split-level house listening to all of his albums and watching videos. We become obsessed with Courtney Love and want to be just like her. We read every interview we can find and cut out every picture, modeling our clothes on hers. We go to Thayer Street, by Brown University, and buy vintage baby-doll dresses and fishnet stockings. I find a pair of deeply discounted Mary Jane-style Doc Martens and beg Dad to buy them for me. I wear them with everything I own.

We troll the CD stores for the Pixies, Sonic Youth, Bikini Kill, and the Sex Pistols, too. We rent *Sid and Nancy* at the video store because Courtney Love has a bit part and we watch it so many times we know every line. That Christmas, Derek gives it to me on VHS and when I unwrap it, I'm so thrilled by the gift that I hug him. He pushes me away. "Whatever," he says. "I just know you like the stupid movie." I squeeze him again, extra hard.

In Barrington, the bands of choice are Phish and the Dave Matthews Band, and I set myself in direct opposition to the boat shoes and white baseball hats of the soccer-playing, Grateful Dead–loving popular kids. That summer as eighth grade ends and my friend and I look forward to high school I imagine all the drama that awaits me. We dye our hair pink and talk about how different things will be. Every book and every movie I've ever seen about high school says this will be the most important time of my life and I'm sure it will. I plan all my outfits with the notion that Courtney Love will come to my school and pick out the coolest person. If that happens, I want to be that girl.

That summer I come across an article where someone mentions the book *A Clockwork Orange*. The next time Dad and I are at the library I check it out. On the drive home he looks at my book and slaps his knee.

"This is one of the few cases," he says, "where the movie is just as good as the book. Maybe even better. Your mom and I saw it in the theater when we were first dating."

"Really?" I ask. "Can we rent it?"

I watch the movie as soon as I got home and then start on the book. Dad and I talk about the British ending versus the American ending and at dinner we drive Ann-Marie crazy by calling all of our food eggy-weggs and doing our best Malcolm McDowell impersonations.

Eventually, she has had enough. "What is it with this movie? It's just some idiot with a stick!"

"Ann-Mo," Dad says, "that is the most salient piece of film criticism I may have ever heard."

By the time high school starts in the fall, I've worked my way through all the counterculture and dystopian literature I can find, starting, of course, with *Brave New World* and *1984*.

"Dad," I say, after finishing the Orwell. "At the end, when he's crying and saying he *loves* Big Brother? Oh my God. It was so good. It was so sad." Dad nods from the leather chair in the living room. He has a giant telephoto lens trained on Taylor, who looks up at both of us drooling and smiling.

"Taylor-Ann!" I say, "Show us your buddies!" Taylor proudly displays her collection of pacifiers—two in each hand. Dad snaps pictures of her. I hold up an issue of *Shutterbug* magazine with a giant thirty-five-millimeter camera on the cover and point at the image.

"Taylor, who's this?"

She focuses on the magazine cover and crawls over to me. "Dada!" she says, punching the image of the camera with her moistened buddy, leaving a smudge. "It's Dada!" Dad and I both clap wildly and Taylor giggles, shoving two of the pacifiers into her mouth.

I spend hours in my bedroom in front of the mirror trying on outfits for school. I like small vintage dresses and ripped fishnet stockings layered over colored tights. I scour the Salvation Army for the perfect old-lady cardigans. I use Manic Panic to dye my hair every few weeks. My favorite thing is to walk through the corridors and hear people whisper (seniors even) about my clothes and hair. I delight in making a spectacle of myself—writing song lyrics on my arms and jeans and talking in a loud British accent. Derek and I hang out at the Dairy Mart up the street from our house and ask older teenagers to buy us cigarettes. At school, I prefer brooding in the girls' room, reading poetry by the Beats, and smoking Camel Lights to going to class. I have detention almost every day.

At home, nobody seems to really notice my bad behavior at school. I want Dad to know what a rebel I was but I can never seem to get his attention.

———◆———

RECENTLY THE *PROVIDENCE Journal* had been bought out by Belo Corp., a big national conglomerate that owns papers and news stations across the country. Dad starts to get more night shifts. He leaves for work around five at night and comes home at two or three in the morning. He's always slept for hours on end, but now we almost never see him awake during the day.

One night when I can't sleep, which is often, I get out of bed and make myself a cup of chamomile tea. I curl up into my position on the living room sofa drinking my tea and reading *Interview with the Vampire*. Dad's car pulls into the driveway. When he walks into the living room, he slumps into the chair across from me.

It's the smell of him that makes me look up. He smells like something rotting. Beneath the Polo cologne, and the

Italian grinder bits all over his suit, and even under the scent of alcohol, there's something else. Something not right. He smells sick in the way hospitals smell sick, or ... I can't quite explain it. He has immediately fallen asleep in the chair, his suit jacket slung over the back, his jaw slack. Something has truly changed in him. He has given up trying to impress us. He doesn't talk anymore about "getting better." He doesn't sit with us while we watch movies and crack jokes that we tell to our friends the next day. When he's home he puts the TV on mute and sleeps, all the time, day or night. We live in the same tiny house but I rarely see him.

YEARS BEFORE ON Sunday, September 15, 1987, the unconscious and bleeding body of Michael P. Metcalf, chairman, chief executive officer, and publisher of the *Providence Journal* and *Evening Bulletin* lay sprawled alongside his bicycle on the road near his summer home in Westport, Massachusetts. One week later, he died from serious head injuries sustained in the apparent freak accident. There were no witnesses to the incident and while the Bristol County medical examiner's autopsy report showed "nothing startling," murmurs of foul play rippled through the state of Rhode Island, pooling at the feet of the usual suspects: the corrupt courts and state officials, and the powerful Patriarca crime family.

His death marked the beginning of the end of an era for the *Providence Journal* and coincided generally with a decline in print journalism nationwide. The Metcalfs had made their fortune in mills and helped endow the esteemed Rhode Island School of Design, but it was with their ownership of the *Providence Journal* that they became a Rhode Island dynasty. On the paper's centennial in 1929, then-publisher Stephen Metcalf declared the paper would last another century if "the emblems of independence and honesty still fly at the masthead, and if no man or group of men permit themselves to sully her honor or integrity for their own personal ends."

With Michael Metcalf at the helm, it seemed the *Journal* would continue not only as a beacon of courageous, locally focused journalism but also as a trusted institution employing hundreds of loyal Rhode Islanders. Indeed, the day of his mysterious accident was an auspicious one for Metcalf: It was the first day the paper would be printed at the new production facility—a gleaming, state-of-the-art project of which he was particularly proud—and the building where my father worked for many years. Having found no paper in his mailbox to inspect, Metcalf biked off down the road to purchase one. What happened next is the stuff of conjecture but one thing is clear: He would never see the *Providence Journal* again.

At its height, the newspaper had seven local bureaus, an astonishing number for a state that can be traversed by car in under an hour. Joel Rawson, who began his career at the *Journal* as a copy editor, rose through the ranks to become editor in chief due in large part to a series of fascinating long-form stories that were often a year or more in the making. The paper implemented intensive writing workshops and "Story of the Week" contests. In 1986, then-editor Charles Hauser was sentenced to an eighteen-month suspended prison term and the paper was fined a hundred thousand dollars for publishing a story about Raymond L. S. Patriarca, based on FBI documents being held under a temporary restraining order. Metcalf stood by the story and his editor, stating that his was a decision "that was made by the newspaper in good faith and in the reasonable belief that the First Amendment justified the publication." It was not the first or last time the Metcalfs butted heads with the mafia and the courts.

It was precisely this type of stubborn rectitude that set the *Journal* apart from other Rhode Island institutions. Criminal exploits and entrenched governmental corruption are hallmarks of this tiny state that bears certain monolithic qualities. Overwhelmingly Catholic, unabashedly corrupt, and with a flair for extravagant provincialism, the state nonetheless came to accept the *Providence Journal* as a kind of moral steward. With a hyperfocus on local journalism, its wealthy Protestant owners—exemplified by Michael Metcalf—demanded honesty and honored public service, paid fair wages, and rewarded loyalty. The *Journal*'s almost priggish commitment to integrity saw returns in the form of prestige, with four Pulitzer Prizes, and financial success. While still under private ownership the paper operated at a healthy profit, which Metcalf used to invest in forward-thinking technologies such as cell towers and the purchase of television stations.

The *Journal* today is a shadow of its formal self. The *Evening Bulletin* edition was cut decades ago. The story of the paper's demise is familiar to most people who have followed the decline of print journalism in the era of the Internet. In 1996, Metcalf's successor took the company public. The initial Providence Journal Company valuation was one hundred million dollars. Just six months later, the majority shareholders elected to sell the company to media conglomerate Belo Corp., based in Dallas, Texas, for a billion and a half dollars. Like most large-scale ventures, Belo was concerned less with the paper itself than with its many assets, including those television stations purchased by Michael Metcalf. On the day of the sale, Elise Metcalf Mauran and Pauline C. Metcalf spoke for the Metcalf family with a full-page ad in the paper that read, "We mourn the sale of the Providence Journal Company to A. H. Belo...we are saddened by the loss of independence of the newspaper and what that has meant for well over 100 years to the citizens of Providence and the State of Rhode Island."

———•———

IN 2009, I contact the journalist, Dean Starkman, who'd been part of a team that won a Pulitzer Prize for covering corruption in Rhode Island. He'd also exposed Peter Gilbert's deal with the state. He was a young reporter at the time and he remembers well a line from the grand jury testimony that he quotes in one of his articles, and that shocked me when I first read it: Gerald Mastracchio choking the life out of my mother and saying, "Come on you rat, give me the death rattle." To him that utterance encapsulates the evil of these men. He can't understand, as an outsider, Rhode Islanders' fascination with organized criminals; he'd wanted to show them for the brutal thugs they were. To him, the *Journal* was one of the only non-corrupt organizations in the state.

For men like my dad, the *Journal* was their whole life. He was exceptionally proud of his job.

As an adult, I write about my conversation with Dean Starkman and about how his stories help me finally approach the truth about my mother. A day after my article is published in the *New York Times* I receive this email:

> Ms. Carroll, it was actually the description of your father's death, not your mother's, that sent a chill down my spine. I was the Chief Financial Officer responsible for negotiating the sale of the Providence Journal. Just after announcing the

deal I was kicked out of the house, the 31-year-old father of two babies, for being a drunk. I didn't see my kids that Christmas of 1996 and, as a result, decided to try to get sober rather than commit suicide. I have been clean for the 13 years since and, like you, have become a writer obsessed with telling the truth no matter how painful. If my actions as CFO at the Journal in any way contributed to your hardship I am deeply and sincerely sorry.

Thomas Matlack

I'm stunned by the message. I wonder what my dad would have made of it. Because in a way, through no malice on his part, Matlack's actions did contribute to my dad's death. The *Journal* was the one place my dad completely belonged, completely fit, and the sale changed all that. Reading the email, I feel it again, the same feeling I'd had in college going through the *Journal*'s online archives: that "lonely impulse of delight."

—■·—

TEN

My freshman year I fail algebra and have to attend summer school in the neighboring town of Bristol to make up the class. I pay attention and quickly work my way through the sections of the course that had mystified me throughout the school year. Suddenly, actually doing the formulas instead of writing song lyrics, the math makes sense. On the night before my final exam in summer school, Dad calls down to the basement from the top of the stairs. I'm surprised to hear his voice.

"Want to go see a movie?" he asks.

I look at the clock. It's after eight. I have to be up for summer school the next day at seven.

"Sure," I say.

In the car Dad taps the dashboard in tune with the music on the radio. "You're going to love this movie," he tells me. "It's fucking amazing." In the lobby of the movie theater, the air-conditioning pumping over us. Dad buys two tickets for *Pulp Fiction*. I've never seen anything like it. On the way home we talk about it nonstop. That night in my room I do an impression of Mia Wallace in my mirror and I'm too excited to get to sleep until almost four in the morning. At seven, Dad knocks on my door to wake me up for school. I drag myself out of bed to take the final test. When it's over, I walk over to Dad's waiting car. "Did you pass?"

"Yeah," I say. "I got an A in the class."

"Good job, kiddo." He slides on a pair of Oakley wrap-around sunglasses and pulls the car out of the high school parking lot. It's the best grade I've gotten on anything all year.

On nights when Ann-Marie has to go out, I take care of Taylor. By now Taylor talks a bit and walks. She moves around in wildly unstable steps, hurling herself forward with the force of her own momentum. She watches *The Lion King* on repeat and has a VHS collection of songs from Disney cartoons. We sit on the living room carpet and sing along to them together.

I put her in her high chair and make an elaborate process of picking what her dinner will be from the jars of baby food lined up in the kitchen cabinet by the refrigerator. What goes better with turkey—mashed peas or mashed green beans? And for dessert—do we want plums or applesauce? Taylor is a happy, giggly baby. She drools constantly, leaving a dark half-moon on the neckline of all her clothes, and loves to poke and kiss Shilo, who lets herself be pinched and slapped by Taylor's clumsy baby hands. It's fascinating to see her go from amorphous infant lump to a real person who expresses her desires for things by pushing an oversize cardboard picture book into your lap, or beckoning through the bars of her crib at the pacifiers just out of her reach.

Most often on the nights I watch Taylor, Dad is gone or asleep in his room, unaware of what's happening in the rest of the house. But some nights, like one intolerably hot August evening, as I put Taylor in the bathtub and try to cool her heat-rash-stricken body with a damp washcloth and she cries and cries, Dad calls from the bedroom.

I look down at Taylor, naked and miserable in her padded chair in the bathtub. I pretend not to have heard him. "Ssssh," I whisper to Taylor and hand her a pacifier. She throws it over the side of the tub and continues to cry.

"Leah," calls Dad.

"What?"

"Bring her in here."

I wrap a thin towel loosely around Taylor and lift her out of the tub, carrying her to her room. We sit in the rocking chair in front of the open window. A box fan whirs loudly by our side.

"Did you hear me?" Dad yells again. "You can bring her in here."

"She's better now," I yell back even though Taylor is still crying.

"Jesus Christ," says Dad. "What do you think I'm going to do to her?"

I sit silent, not moving from the rocking chair. Eventually Taylor drifts off to sleep and Dad is quiet in his room. I don't know what he'd do to her, but I do know that she's the most precious thing to me in the world. And I know Dad has turned some kind of corner.

———•———

FOR MY BIRTHDAY that year, Dad takes me to Thayer Street to get my nose pierced. I sat in a dentist's chair while the piercer lines up his silver needles on a paper napkin. I pick out a small steel hoop decorated with a tiny ball. Dad insists on taking pictures during the whole process and I'm mortified until the piercer, tattoos flexing beneath his white T-shirt, admires Dad's camera and asks to look at it. I sit, so excited about getting my nose pierced that I can barely breathe, while Dad and the man bond over the superiority of Canon lenses. By the time they've begun listing the litany of reasons that Morrissey is a whiny ass-hole, I think I might cry from anticipation. Dad looks over at me, pulls the camera to his eye, and says, "Well, it's probably time to put a hole in her face." He moves around me snapping away as the man slides a needle into my cartilage.

"It was fun, Dad!" I say when it's all over. I admire my nose ring in the car mirror. "Like it hurt but it was a good kind of hurt, you know?"

"Good Lord," says Dad. "Just promise me you won't get any tattoos." Dad always says that people are surprised he doesn't smoke or have tattoos. My Aunt Rita explained to me once that growing up, their mom made sure they had the nicest clothes and the shiniest shoes. She taught them how to present themselves to the world. Being a Vietnam vet and a man who hangs out in bars, his intense dislike of tattoos and cigarettes does seem a bit out of character, but if you really know him, if you know the line he walks between who he is and who he wants to be, it makes perfect sense.

"Uh-huh," I say, watching the way my nose ring looks when I talk, or look slightly to the left. I'm definitely the coolest person in high school, I think.

━━━━━━━━

MY SOPHOMORE YEAR I have a boyfriend. He has a blue Ford hatchback, in which we drive around Barrington looking for stuff to do. It's not long before I figure out I don't like Dave very much—not just as a boyfriend, but as a person in general. He steals blank checks from his mother, who is disabled by multiple sclerosis, and shows me how he makes them out to Cash. Of course I don't object when the stolen money keeps us in cigarettes, Dunkin' Donuts coffee, and Bickford's meals.

It isn't the theft itself that bothers me. It's more the methodically shitty way in which he conducts his schemes. He is, I realize, no good, and not in the hippie-burnout way that people assume. Rather, he's the kind of just-smart-enough criminal who will likely spend a lot of time in prison for petty crimes as an adult.

As much as I'm pretty much continuously disgusted and annoyed by him, we stay together for my entire sophomore year. I like the freedom of his car. He begs to come over late at night after Dad and Ann-Marie have gone to bed, and I acquiesce, apathetically French-kissing him for a few minutes at a time. I wonder if I'll ever have a boyfriend that I like.

THAT WINTER, AS Belo restructures, my father is laid off. The *Journal* pays him a generous severance and gives him access to his 401(k), but it's as if a lifeline has been severed. Before there'd been an excuse to get out of bed, at least for the hours he had to be at work. Now there isn't. I can't imagine my dad not working at the *Journal*. What will he do? When he gets out of bed to take pictures or do whatever it is he does on his own, he puts on his natty suits and shoes and overcoats. Then he comes home and falls heavily into bed, still wearing his expensive clothes as he tosses and turns in front of the muted TV.

One morning he offers to drive Derek and me to school. Once we're in the car it's clear something is very wrong. Inside the Mitsubishi it smells like something died. The drive from our house to school is less than three-quarters of a mile but Dad pulls the car over to vomit on the way. Derek opens his rear door and just gets out, heading down the sidewalk to school. I unbuckle my seat belt and tell Dad I'll walk the rest of the way as well.

"I'm fine," he wipes his mouth with his hand.

"It's okay," I say. "We're practically there." Then I slip out of the car before he can say anything else. As I walk around the hood to get to the sidewalk on the opposite side of the street, I glance down at the puddle of vomit on the ground. It's pink and foamy, as if he has been throwing up blood.

———•———

WEEKS LATER, WHEN I come home from Dave's house, Ann-Marie is waiting up for me.

"Your father and I are getting a divorce," she says.

Her contacts are out for the night and she has on her large glasses and white sweatpants. "I've decided that you can come and stay with us," she says. "If you want. It's your decision."

When she says "us," I realize she's talking about Taylor and Derek. I don't want to be without my sister.

"Okay," I say, right away.

I try to summon the appropriate emotion but can't figure out what it should be. Their divorce seems inevitable. For the last year they've barely talked. Dad has cut himself off from all of us and is drunk all the time. When he lost his job we all doubted he'd really try to find a new one. Ann-Marie explains that we'll move to the apartment building her parents own, the one she lived in when she and Dad first met. They'll sell our house. Dad will have to find an apartment to live in. When she's done talking I go to my room and try to cry. I think if I can cry I'll figure out how I should feel about the whole thing. I think if I cry, it will make me a better daughter for abandoning my dad. But I can't cry, no matter how much I screw up my face and heave my gut, trying to force out emotion.

That weekend, as I pour myself cereal in the kitchen, Dad comes in. His silver hair is a crazy mess around his head. He leans against the kitchen sink and puts his palms behind him on the counter. "Well kiddo," he says, "looks like it's just you and me again."

My stomach flops. I was sure that he and Ann-Marie had talked about who would go with whom.

"I'm going to live with Ann-Marie." I avoid eye contact. "She asked me to, so I thought you wanted me to," I add quickly.

"Oh," says Dad. He walks from the kitchen to his room, and slams the door shut so hard that all his framed photos on the wall rattle.

For the next few weeks as we pack up our stuff in boxes and stack them along the wall in the kitchen, Dad ignores me. He won't look at me or speak to me. It's one thing if he's sleeping, like he always does, but to actively act as if I'm not there is something I've never experienced. I try talking to him about what I'm reading, about what he thinks about a certain band, but my questions are met with a determined silence, as the boxes pile higher and our move date gets closer.

———————

ANN-MARIE STARTS DATING almost as soon as we move out, and I babysit for Taylor more and more. Fifteen, with no job and no money, I take Taylor for long walks in her stroller down to the Barrington River. I remember being little and walking with my grandmother around her little cul-de-sac and how it always made me happy. As spring comes and with it that old creeping anxiety I get with the changes of the seasons, I hope the walks with Taylor might make me feel better. But my stomach still turns nervously as I push her stroller down these new suburban streets and along the murky edge of the river where we collect pebbles and broken bits of clamshell. I'm nervous all the time, it seems, but I'm never sure why.

Our downstairs neighbors in the apartment building are a family of five, three small children, their mother, and their father, Doc. Ann-Marie quickly begins dating Doc's friend Marco. Marco is young and handsome, with black hair and brown eyes and a thick mustache and beard. He has a small commercial fishing boat, a clam dragger, and he gathers up quahogs from the ocean floor. He brings them home, and we boil the clams in a stockpot with potatoes and Saugys. He's nice enough, and seems to like Ann-Marie, but it's clear he has spent his life dragging for shellfish and not necessarily getting an education. Trying to connect with Derek one night he offers to take him out on the boat, promising he'll be able to make lots of "moneys."

"Money," Derek says.

"Yeah," says Marco, "that's what I said. Moneys. You can make lots of moneys."

"You can't say moneys," says Derek. "It's not plural. You make *money*."

Marco, perplexed, tries to brush off Derek's tone. "I'm just saying, if you wanted..."

It quickly becomes apparent, however, that Marco's lack of education isn't his major flaw. At night sitting on the couch with Ann-Marie while we watch TV, or at the dinner table while we eat oyster stew, he trails off mid-sentence into quiet gibberish. His eyelids droop once, twice, three times until finally his chin comes to rest against his chest and he starts snoring.

"Marco's on heroin," I tell Ann-Marie as she shakes him by the shoulder.

"He is *not!*" she says.

We're sitting at the dining table. From where I am, I can see out over the backyard—a rectangle of patchy grass set off from the gravel parking lot by a series of railroad ties. Across from me at the table, Marco's head bobs up and down. Taylor sits happily in her booster seat playing with a pile of oyster crackers. She and Marco are occupying the same mental space, some different place from Ann-Marie and me.

"Then why does he nod out all the time?" I ask.

"He's tired," says Ann-Marie. "He fishes all day."

Marco's upper body flops face-first onto the table, just missing the bowl of soup. He snores contentedly on the vinyl place mat. I smirk at Ann-Marie. She stands up and strokes his head. He opens his eyes and smiles at her, his head sideways on the table, but doesn't sit up.

"Well, what the hell do you know about heroin anyway, smart-ass?" asks Ann-Marie.

It's a good question and one that, wisely, I don't answer, despite my natural inclination to be the expert of all things. Toward the end of that school year my loser boyfriend has gotten into snorting heroin, because he decides pot makes him paranoid. I drive with him to the Manton Heights Housing Project in Providence where he buys the drugs. Before pulling in, Dave will have me rifle through the pile of cassette tapes on the passenger-side floor.

"Find the Beastie Boys," he'll say. "We need them to know we're cool with them." Then we pull up to a corner in his hatchback, the rear window all but covered in

Grateful Dead stickers, white-boy rap blaring from the crappy speakers in the tape deck.

At first Dave only snorts the heroin instead of shooting it, but he has a friend Lindsay who regularly shoots up. Lindsay is infamous in Barrington. The summer before I started high school, there had been MISSING CHILD posters of her taped to telephone poles and hung in storefronts across town. She'd gone to a Phish show and run off with a group of kids for months. Now back in Barrington, she seems to me the most world-wise teenager I've ever met. And she's an honest-to-goodness heroin addict at seventeen, having already gone unsuccessfully to rehab and to treatment at a methadone clinic.

The three of us go together to buy heroin, which I never do because I'm too scared. Lindsay has a tiny scrappy voice and talks in slang I do my best to imitate. Looking up at Dave beneath a mop of matted hair, she'll smile sweetly and blink her large dark eyes. "Dave," she'll say, "let's get some diesel. I wanna get high."

She carries a syringe in her enormous canvas army bag and shoots up in the backseat of Dave's car. Once when she can't locate a vein in her arm, she asks if someone will hold her wrist tightly so she can shoot into a vein in her hand. I volunteer right away, squeezing her wrist tightly so that her veins puff up big and blue.

Later Dave tells me that I didn't have to do that, that Lindsay sometimes makes people uncomfortable, and that I don't have to do anything I don't want to. I don't explain to him that I'd never do the drug, but that I think being around it is cool and that Lindsay is way more of an authentic junkie than Dave will ever be.

I try to impress Lindsay with stories about my mom that are mostly made up.

"We used to have junkies stay at our house all the time," I tell her once. "One time one of them ate his own puke on a bet for money to get high."

Lindsay nods as if this is something she's witnessed many a time. I try to conjure a narrative of what it had been like being the child of an addict mother, but really I remember mostly brief and benign glimpses of my mom. Her silhouette in the open door, her hanging strips of film from the shower rod, her brushing back my sweaty hair when I must have had a fever. I can't really see her in any of these memories. There's just the sense that she's there.

But for all my efforts, Lindsay seems most impressed by the fact that I don't do heroin.

"You're really smart," she says to me once. "You don't act like these other dumb Barrington girls. Like, obviously you're smart because you don't do dope and stuff. But you are really smart about books and things, too."

———•———

I MISS DAD. When we spend time together it starts out awkward, but then we go to a movie or up to Boston to take pictures, and we have things to talk about. On the hour-long drives back from Boston, Dad tells me about things like this new show he has been watching on Comedy Central called *The Daily Show,* and how funny it is. In between the times we see each other, in the days before Google, I save up questions about things that are in the news to ask Dad, later.

He explains the centuries-old conflict in Bosnia to me and why hopes for any kind of resolution without understanding the history are pointless and shortsighted. We talk about Clinton's Don't Ask, Don't Tell policy. I've recently joined the brand-new gay/straight alliance at my high school. Dad explains that it's akin to a Jim Crow law, something separate but equal and therefore not really equal at all. "What's Jim Crow?" I ask, and then recite his answer nearly verbatim to anybody who will listen for the next few months.

On one of our outings I tell Dad how unhappy I am at school and how much I want to transfer. Dad agrees that School One, an alternative school in Providence, seems like a good fit for me and takes me on an appointment to interview with the faculty and take the placement tests. In my interview with Dad and the principal, Dad smiles charmingly at the woman and crosses his heel over his knee, leaning backward to rest his hand on the back of the chair.

"I've thought for a long time that Leah and public school are a bad fit," he tells the principal. "I mean, this is a kid who reads Goethe in her free time." The closest I've come to reading Goethe is when I asked Dad what Faust was and who "Geth" was, while reading Anne Rice, but the principal is so impressed I don't dare contradict him. She escorts us out, handing over a large manila envelope of financial aid information for Dad to fill out. She beams at me as we walk out onto the sidewalk. "I'm really looking forward to getting to know you better, Leah!" she says. In the car I look into the envelope. There are a bunch of tax forms that Dad, as my legal custodial parent, will have to fill out. "You'll do it, right?" I ask.

"Of course," he says. "I think this is really good move for you. You need a place like this, I think."

Over the next few weeks I abandon any semblance of finishing up my sophomore year with passing grades. I tell everyone that it doesn't matter because I'm going to School One. But soon the school starts calling, saying they haven't received Dad's paperwork. The next time I see him I ask him about it.

"Oh yeah," he says. "I have it. I just haven't mailed it in." As the summer comes and goes I realize I'll be going back to Barrington High School in the fall.

"My dad is so fucked up!" I whine to Dave. We sit on the front porch of my three-family house, smoking ciga-rettes. "I hate Barrington. He just doesn't want to fill out tax forms. It's so unfair." I flick my cigarette onto the street and light another one. I puff angrily and exhale into the thick summer air, cicadas buzzing loudly all around us. I think about Dad and how it always seems like he drinks more in the summer and becomes more dangerous. I'm furious with him. I turn to Dave. "If something ever happens to me," I say, "my dad probably did it. I've been afraid before that he would murder all of us." I stare hard at Dave, daring him to doubt the conviction of my statement.

"Yeah," says Dave. "But I always kind of thought your dad might kill himself. Since you didn't go and live with him and stuff."

I reach over and pinch Dave's arm, twisting his skin between my fingers as hard as I can. "Ow!" he whines. "What are you doing?"

"I fucking hate you," I say. And I do. I hate his big black cow eyes with their long lashes and his slender nonthreatening limbs and the stupid poetry he writes me, where instead of saying "you" he says "thou" and "thee." And I hate that this ridiculous person would dare to insinuate that somehow my dad is not strong enough to go on with life. He has never met my dad. He doesn't know his booming laugh, or how he'd worked his way through the seven-volume Shelby Foote history of the Civil War in a single month of intense concentration, or the way that people cluster around him to hear his stories at the bar, or how people cower if he just looks at them a certain way, with a certain turn of his body, and a certain tilt of his face. He wasn't there the other Saturday morning in Dunkin' Donuts, like I was, when a woman held up a long line of people by going back and forth on what choices to include in her dozen donuts until finally, exasperated, my dad called out from the middle of line, "Lady, they're just

fucking donuts," and the whole store erupted in spontane-
ous applause.

Fuck this kid, I think, and walk back into the house,
locking the door behind me. From the street Dave calls my
name and weeps loudly until one of the neighbors sticks
his head out of a window and threatens to call the cops.

I'm done with him. Done with his heroin snorting and
doing nothing but riding around in his car and listening
to terrible live Grateful Dead shows on his tape deck. I'm
mortified by the way I've taken to wearing hippie clothes
and singing along to Phish songs to fit in with him. But no
matter how much I try, I can't be done with the idea he has
planted, the idea that my dad might hurt himself, and that
if he does, it will be all my fault.

———

I SULK MY way through my junior year of high school,
failing so epically and unequivocally that the assistant
principal points out how I easily could channel just some
of that negative energy into passing at least one class. I
scoff at him.

We've always worn off-brand clothes, purchased on lay-
away, but now with only Ann-Marie's income, there is no
money for anything new; Ann-Marie no longer buys us
"school clothes." So my wardrobe is almost entirely com-
prised of Salvation Army finds that I alter on the sewing
machine Grandma Ann buys for me. During classes I
sketch out patterns for skirts and dresses. I spend hours

sewing a long dress with bell sleeves that becomes my favorite. I buy six different types of scrap fabric, cut them into large triangles, and sew them into a pair of Salvation Army corduroys—it's a version of a popular trend in my high school of taking straight-legged pants and turning them into wide-legged ones. I love making my own clothes. My room is scattered with long strips of ragged ribbon I've salvaged from a craft store liquidation sale, musty piles of old cardigans and skirts that I buy on blue-tag days at the Salvation Army and think I might repurpose, and, much to Taylor and Ann-Marie's continued annoyance, straight pins and spools of thread that tangle around our ankles and stab the soles of our feet.

I start to hang out with a group of girls, and the five of us, Reba, Alex, Heather, Sarah, and I, form an unlikely but inseparable alliance. Reba and Heather are clearly headed to the Ivy League, but we still spend our nights and weekends parked at Barrington Beach smoking cigarettes and creating derisive nicknames for all the people in our high school. I laugh harder sitting in Alex's little black Honda Civic than I ever have before as a teenager.

My friends' families became a support system for me. Heather's parents stock their basement fridge with microwave burritos and cans of Dr Pepper for when I come over after school. Reba's parents encourage my writing and pay me to take photographs for them. Alex drives me everywhere, to and from school, to my part-time job at the supermarket, and to doctor and dentist appointments. The group of us confess everything to each other, conducting mini therapy sessions on the beach late at night while sipping from a bottle of vodka. Alex feels terribly out of place, Reba feels she has too much to live up to, and Heather wonders why old friends are now mean to her. And of course we are all madly, wildly, and unrequitedly in love with boys.

The summer after my junior year, I go to an outdoor music festival with my friend Rick and we meet up with some guys from school. John, who is a grade younger than us, is with them. It's a beautiful day, hot and sunny, and the concert takes place at a campground. We smoke pot and strip to our underpants and go swimming in the freezing-cold pool at the edge of the tents. Normally, I'm embarrassed by my body. I'm barely an A cup and at five foot five I weigh less than a hundred pounds. I have the long, gangly arms and legs of a praying mantis. But that day, something is different—I feel calm and confident for one of the only times I can remember. Nobody has seen me in just my underwear since I was a child, including my ex-boyfriend. Later, after borrowing a giant T-shirt from one of the guys who is camping out, I see that my camisole top has been neatly laid out to dry.

"Thanks, Rick," I say to my friend, oddly touched that he has taken the time, when I would have thrown the shirt in a ball on the ground and probably forgotten about it.

"I didn't do it," he says. "John did."

I'm stunned. John is by far the handsomest boy I've ever

seen in my life. He's on the soccer team and doesn't smoke cigarettes and I'm sure he doesn't really even know who I am.

"Oh," I say, watching John and a friend kick a Hacky Sack to each other.

As the sun sets, Rick trades some of the quarter pound of pot he has brought with him for a sheet of acid.

"It's white blotter," he says. "I don't even know if it's real." We all divvy it up generously, sure it won't work. An hour later I am—as I keep repeating over and over to Rick and then collapsing into giggles—"tripping face, man." I find myself in a stand of trees, clutching a warm Miller High Life, engaged in a passionate discussion with John about colors and what they *really* mean. Later we make our way over to where a reggae band plays. I look up at the crystal-clear night sky and when I look back down, the stars are suddenly all around my body and I can move them around with my hands. I sit down in the middle of all the dancing people and stare up at the moon. A shadow moves slowly across its surface until eventually all I can see is a ring of beautiful white fire at its edges. Then the shadow dissolves.

I turn to John. "Did you just see the lunar eclipse?"

He sits down next to me and shakes his head no. "Are you cold?" he asks. I don't respond. He unties a button-down shirt from around his waist and I drape it across my shoulders and almost die from swooning so hard.

When it's time to leave, Rick and I get into his brown

two-door car that sits ominously low to the ground. We're both still incredibly high. I've smoked more pot that night than I ever have in my life and I'm not even close to coming down off the LSD, which at some point I decided to take more of. Rick still has some of the acid and a giant bag of pot on him.

"I should carry that stuff for you," I say. "Male cops can't search women." We both agree this a good idea. Driving down the pitch-black roads from Exeter to Barrington feels like being in video game come to life, and I cling to the sides of the passenger seat as we weave our way around curves. At one point, I see a long line of lights in what seems like the middle of the road. Unlike the lunar eclipse, which only I could see, Rick sees the lights and pulls off to the side of the road

"How will we get around it?" he asks.

We stare and stare and finally realize the lights are headlights, and the floating line is an overpass. All we have to do is drive underneath it. We congratulate one another on keeping it together.

I wake the next morning still wearing John's button-down shirt. I wander into Derek's room. My body feels slimy from the acid but I can't stop smiling. I sit down in the big orange chair Derek had found on the sidewalk and lugged up to his room.

"How was the show?" he asks.

"Derek," I say, "I am totally in love." I absentmindedly pat the front pocket of my shirt and feel something puffy. I pull out a giant bag of pot and the cellophane wrapper from a pack of cigarettes containing a strip of blotter paper. I hold them both in my lap and start laughing.

"Whoa," says Derek. He's just waking up and his dark hair, so similar to mine that people often assume we're biological siblings, sticks out in all directions. I'm glad, like always, to have Derek there. We fight but really he knows me better than anyone else. We've lived in the same houses, shared the same bathrooms, and for so long that I never think of him as just a "step" brother.

The girls' reaction to my newfound love is more high pitched. I showed them John's shirt and ask their advice on how I should go about returning it. We squeal at the various possibilities and drive past his house several times, once even pulling into the driveway, as I scream at Alex to drive away. I don't see him for the rest of the summer, but they indulge my rattling on about how perfect and amazing he is. Now when we get one of Alex's friends from the gas station where she works to go to the liquor store for us, my beer of choice is Miller High Life. The group of us sits on a narrow rocky outcropping of the beach and drink it while I recount my amazing discussion with John about colors. Of course, the girls are the ones I really love, the ones who look out for me, and laugh with me, and see the potential inside me that I don't.

<hr />

I DON'T SEE Dad most of that summer, but shortly before school starts again, he calls me. I answer the phone in the kitchen, wrapping the cord around my wrist and looking out the window at the driveway. Doc, the downstairs neighbor, is draped across one of our chaise lounges with his eyes closed. His four-year-old daughter goes up and down Taylor's plastic play slide next to him.

"I was thinking we could go to DC for a few days," Dad says over the phone.

"Okay," I say. The last time we'd seen each other we had discussed the recently opened Holocaust Museum.

"We'll drive through the night and get there in the morning. It takes about eight hours. Do you want to go?"

"Yeah," I say, and then catching my monosyllabic responses add, "I want to see the Holocaust Museum."

"Me too," says Dad. "I think it's important that you see the Vietnam Wall, too. I'll pick you up tomorrow night? Around ten?"

"That sounds good." As I'm hanging up I hear Dad clear his throat.

"Love you," he says.

"Yeah," I say, caught off guard. I hang up without saying it back. Should I call him back and tell him I love him too? I unwind the phone cord from my wrist and decide it would be too weird. I walk down the back staircase and out onto the patch of grass behind the house.

"Can I bum a cigarette?" I ask Doc. He opens his eyes and looks at me, his pupils tiny pin pricks. High on heroin, I realize.

"Hey, beautiful," he says. His voice sounds stuffed up,

like he has a cold. He reaches beside him and takes out a cigarette from the beat-up-looking pack of Basics at his side. "Do you need a light?" he asks.

I stand for a moment, cigarette balanced between two fingers. I can still hear the sound of Dad clearing his throat. I feel ashamed.

"Please," I say.

Doc stands and lights my cigarette. I exhale and lean against the house, conscious of the way I look and hold my cigarette. I can sense that Doc is looking at me, and it makes me embarrassed. I slouch a bit against the wooden shingles. I wish I'd stayed upstairs.

"Nice night, isn't it?" Doc's jeans sit low on his narrow hips and I look away quickly from the strip of tanned flesh exposed beneath his T-shirt. Then, suddenly, he's in front of me, balancing his palms against the side of the house and pinning me between his arms. I try to slip out from beneath him and he grinds his pelvis into mine. "Nice night," he says again, eyes closed.

I push him away and run up the stairs. When I get to my door I realize I'm still holding the lit cigarette. Disgusted, I throw it into the kitchen sink and run to my room. I sit there in the encroaching darkness, sweating in the stuffy space. I feel like if I try to stand up I won't be able to.

———•———

DAD PICKS ME up the next night around ten. I'd been lying on the yellowing white leather sofa in the living room, wondering if I should have agreed to go at all. It had been a long time since I'd spent more than twenty-four hours with him. What if it didn't go well and I was trapped on an eight-hour car ride away from home? I heard his car horn outside and gathered my bag of stuff. Ann-Marie's room was dark. She and Taylor were staying at her new boy-friend's house.

Dad drives a black five-speed Jetta. After he totaled the Mitsubishi, he'd driven a big Pontiac for a while, but he must have stopped making the payments on it at some point, because a large man had come pounding on the door to our apartment and demanding that Ann-Marie tell him where the car was. After she'd explained to him that they were divorced and she didn't know, I asked her who he had been.

"The fucking repo man," she said.

Now, Dad pops the trunk for me and I throw my over-night bag in and get into the passenger seat. Right away I can tell Dad had been drinking. The scent of whiskey and Polo permeates the car.

"Hey kiddo," he says.

I slump in my seat and make a big show of buckling my seat belt. "How long will it take us to get there?"

"About eight hours," says Dad. "You can sleep in the back if you want."

"Can I drive?" I have my license but we only have Ann-Marie's one car and she doesn't let me use it, so I never get to drive.

"Why not?" says Dad. "The highway's easy." He pulls off onto the side of 95 and we get out of the car and run around the front to switch positions. Cars fly past me in the dark as I jump into the driver's seat and slam the door shut. Dad talks me through guiding the car into fifth gear and the car rattles along the dirt shoulder, as I rev the engine and grind gears. Once I'm going fast enough Dad looks behind him and yells, "Go!" I don't even look to my left as I pull onto the highway, heart racing.

"Good job," he says. "Easy from here on out, just stay in fifth. And I'm not drunk, you know." I know he is, but I also know he's not as drunk as he could be, and that means something. I looked straight ahead at the highway in front of me and don't say anything in response. After hours of driving and another stop on the highway to switch spots, so I can climb into the backseat and sleep for a bit, we get into Washington, DC, a little bit after sunrise.

We pull into the hotel parking lot just outside the city in Northern Virginia. Despite how early it is, it's already blazing hot. We emerge from the air-conditioned car onto the blistering asphalt of the parking lot. I pull my bag from the trunk and Dad bends over the backseat of the car, rifling through a pile of laundry for a clean shirt.

"Leah," Dad says, jogging after me. "Jesus Christ, wait up."

As we check in, the woman behind the counter greets us in a thick Southern accent. I've never heard one outside a movie before and when we walk back outside to go to our room, I joke about it with Dad.

"We're in the South now, baby," he says.

"We are?" I've never thought of Washington, DC, as being "the South."

"Well, we're in Virginia," he says. "You'll see."

We throw our stuff in the room and wash our faces and then go to eat breakfast in the hotel lobby. I push my plate down the buffet line and scoop myself a large helping of oatmeal. I join Dad at a table and take a bite of cantaloupe. I hadn't realized how starving the night of driving has made me. Dad looks at a map he's picked up at the front desk.

"We could do the Holocaust Museum first," he says. "And then maybe come back and take a nap. We can go to the Mall tonight. I'd like to get pictures of the Wall at sunset."

I nod, devouring the food on my plate. I scoop a huge spoonful of oatmeal into my mouth, gag, and look up desperately at Dad. He turns away from the map, sees the look on my face and the mound of food on my plate, and laughs out loud.

"Spit it out, kiddo," he says, handing me a napkin. "What's the matter? You never had grits before? I told you we were in the South!"

I do my best to spit the strange rubbery stuff into the napkin, then swallow an entire glass of water trying to get the taste out of my mouth. Dad is still laughing.

"I thought it was oatmeal." It's all I can do to keep from wiping my tongue with the napkin.

"People love that shit," says Dad. "When I got back from Vietnam, they promised to send me to a base near home and I wound up in fucking Alabama. In the middle of fucking July. It was as hot as this at night. And man when they served grits those Southern boys would go wild!"

I push my plate away and smile at Dad. "They're disgusting," I say.

"Yes they are, Leah, daughter of mine. Yes they are."

We leave for the Holocaust Museum after breakfast. By that time, midmorning, the pavement practically sizzles. We wait, the car idling sluggishly at the traffic light, both of us halfheartedly acknowledging the Federal Treasury as we watch for the signal change. It's so hot that in the barely moving traffic the air-conditioning struggles to work. When we finally get into the cool dark museum, we both breathe an audible sigh of relief. Dad nudges me with his shoulder.

"Seems like there is probably something wrong with being psyched to get into the Holocaust Museum because of the air-conditioning, don't you think? I mean the ovens and all?" He raises his eyebrows at me. I roll my eyes but I'm trying not to laugh.

We make our way through the winding, stark design of the place. We look at the chart the Nazis used to determine purity: both parents Aryan, blond hair, blue eyes, the most pure; both parents Jewish, dark hair, dark eyes, the least.

"There's you," Dad says, pointing at a row near the bottom. "Mother Jewish, dark hair, dark eyes." I look up at him thinking he might make a joke, but the look on his face is sad and angry. I wondered if he's thinking about me dying. I wonder if he's thinking about my mom. Had she lived, I would have been raised an observant Jew. I wonder if Dad feels bad about not having done that.

Outside, we stand on the sidewalk with the Jetta's doors cracked, waiting for the heat inside to dissipate slightly before we get back in.

"You should see *Fiddler on the Roof*," Dad says. It comes out like it's something he has been thinking about for a long time.

"Okay," I say. "Is it coming to Providence?"

"If it does," he says, "you should see it with your aunt and your grandmother. I think they would really like it." In the car, Dad adjusts the air-conditioning vent, leaning close to it. His face is bright red. I notice how purple and puffy the lines on his nose and cheeks have become. They made his skin look fragile and sore, and I have the sudden urge to ask him if they hurt. "I need a nap," he says. "That wore me out."

We go back to the hotel and Dad lies down on the bed near the window. We're both glistening with sweat just from the walk from the parking lot to our hotel door. "Did you bring a bathing suit?" Dad asks. "There's a pool."

I hadn't brought one.

"Maybe I'll go in my clothes?" I say to Dad. I think maybe if he wants time to be able to drink, it's now. I change into a giant tie-dyed T-shirt and a pair of army pants I've cut into shorts that go to my knees. I cinch them at my waist with a giant safety pin.

"That's what you're going to swim in?" asks Dad, when I emerge from the bathroom.

"So what?" I say, instantly defensive.

"No big deal," he says. "You might as well just wear one of those Victorian things with the striped arms and legs. I mean are you sure you've got enough on? I can see your ankles." Dad has the ability to see exactly what my specific insecurity is and needle me about it. And I have no ability to disguise emotion on my face. I think of the girls at school sunning themselves on Barrington Beach in their bikinis. I look down at my legs. They're so white they're practically blue and covered in the dark stubble that develops if I don't shave them every single morning. Other girls, I'm sure, are born with golden down on their arms and legs that requires little maintenance. Dad sees the look on my face. "Hey," he says, "I was just joking around with you. You look fine. Don't forget to grab a towel."

There's only one other family inside the gated pool. The young mother and father bob around the shallow end as their daughter swims between them, every limb encased in a blow-up floatie. She looks less like a toddler and more like an inflatable raft. The mom and dad call to her in baby voices and clap their hands. A listless-looking teenage boy sits in the lifeguard chair, looking out at the highway that runs in front of the motel. I lower myself into the deep end and submerge my body, holding on to the bottom hem of my oversize shirt as I drop to the bottom. When I open my eyes underwater I see the blurry outlines of the parents' legs, jumping up and down. I move my hands around in front of my face in the blue water. I love swimming pools. I wish I had a bathing suit.

Walking back to the hotel room, dripping wet, I squeeze out the T-shirt and ball the heavy canvas fabric of the shorts into my fist, trying to dry out a little before I go back into the room. A few doors down a maid in a blue-and-white uniform knocks on a door and then props it open. Her cart of towels and sheets blocks the doorway. I walk down to her and peek my head into the darkened room.

"Excuse me," I say. "Excuse me." She comes to the door and I gesture to my sopping clothes. "Can I have another towel?" I ask. She stares at me. In the silence I can hear myself dripping water onto the pavement. Finally, she shakes her head and hands me a towel. I press it against myself like a squeegee.

I go to our door and knock. I don't want to surprise Dad in the middle of anything. Maybe he's drinking, or watching porn on TV, which I'd caught him doing a few times growing up. I blush just at the word *porn* and try to tell myself I'm being silly. But even with the key card in my soaking pocket, I won't go into the room until Dad opens the door.

Once he does, I stand in the air-conditioning and shiver as Dad turns on the TV.

"How was it?" he asks.

"It was really nice," I say. "It's so hot."

Dad flips through the channels. "I thought we could get dinner in Georgetown," he says. "It's a really cool part of the city, kind of like Thayer Street. I think you'll like it."

I nod and sit down at the edge of the bed.

"Maybe you should take a shower and put on new clothes?"

"Oh," I said dumbly. "Okay."

I come out of the bathroom, towel around my hair, fully dressed. I feel clean and sleepy. Dad sits at the edge of the bed and counts a large pile of twenty-dollar bills. He has never carried a wallet or money clip and loves to have as much cash on hand as possible. His favorite thing is to pull a fat wad of money from his pocket and wave it in front of Derek and me. He has done it so many times for a laugh that by now it makes me embarrassed just thinking about it. I wonder where he's getting his money now that he doesn't have a job. He taps the bills into a neat pile, folds them in half, and puts them into the pocket of the suit pants he has changed into.

"Have you ever seen this show?" he asks, pointing at the TV. I haven't.

"Oh you'd really like it," he says. "It's called *Homicide* and it takes place in Baltimore and it's all based on this book about homicide detectives. The book is great. You should read it. Baltimore—it's like no other city. We should stop there on the way back, do you want to?"

I haven't been with Dad for this long—almost twenty-four hours straight now—since he and Ann-Marie got divorced. Listening to him talk, telling me what books and movies to see, what he has just read about in a magazine article, is my sole understanding of culture outside Barrington. I want to see Baltimore and I want to read *Homicide* and I want to eat dinner in Georgetown. And I want to do all those things with Dad. But I start to feel panicky, like the trip will never end. Like I'll never get back to the Dunkin' Donuts parking lot in Alex's car, where we'll smoke cigarettes and drink enormous coffees, while I talk haughtily about the awesome book I've just read about homicide detectives.

It's as if I want all this to have happened already. I want the memory of it, but the doing it is hard for me. I don't know how to talk to Dad anymore, whether to try to be his peer or to reach all the way back and try again to be his daughter. Every answer I give feels not good enough. So I err on the side of caution.

"We could go," I say, trying to sound noncommittal, and see the look of disappointment flash briefly across his face. He's disappointed in *me*, I realize. Disappointed that I can't just let it all go and have fun, after all the time he has spent planning. Next time, I promise myself, I will say the right thing. I will answer the right way.

At dinner in Georgetown we sit at an outdoor table. I feel drab next to Dad in his immaculate button-down shirt, his silver hair brushed away from his face. Even the veins tracking across his face seem distinguished in the late-day light as he squeezes a lime into his glass of club soda. I order an iced tea, unsweetened, and resist the urge to mix in a packet of sugar.

"I'd like to get pictures of the Wall at sunset," Dad says. Next to our table is his enormous camera bag, his tripod anchored at the bottom of it with Velcro. "We can do some shopping first. On the way back to the car."

I nod my head enthusiastically. Am I being too enthusiastic?

"I really like it here," I say. "Georgetown is really cool."

We walk past boutiques and coffee shops on the way back. Dad looks over his shoulder at me on the narrow sidewalk. "Do you see someplace you want to stop?"

I shrug, trying not to look too eager. "I mean, this place looks cool," I say. We're standing outside a high-end head shop and in the window is a display of necklaces made out of sterling silver, semiprecious stones, and what appear to be delicate bones, all strung together. I think they are the most beautiful things I've ever seen.

Inside, I browse through the small section of CDs, and

slowly make my way over to the jewelry. I'm not used to asking for things but the necklaces are so pretty, I know I will think about them nonstop after we leave. I pick up one from the felt display case and hold it up to my neck. The little cylinders of bone hold in place a teardrop-shaped piece of turquoise, all filigreed at the edge in sterling silver. The stone hangs perfectly, right in the hollow of my neck. "These are kind of cool," I say. "Do you think?"

"Sure," says Dad. "Why don't you pick out two?"

I hold my breath and try to suppress a smile, thinking of how cool the necklaces are, and how I've gotten them, brand-new, in a fancy shop far away from Rhode Island, and how that will always make them special. As the cashier rings them up, Dad and I look at the display of stickers on the wall behind him. I'm giddy with the rush of the purchase, and laugh aloud at the two with black-and-white images, one of older Elvis, and one of young Elvis beneath which are emblazoned the words: I'M DEAD.

"Should I get fat Elvis or skinny Elvis?" asks Dad.

"Fat Elvis," I say. "It's awesome." The cashier slips it into the paper bag with my necklaces. Driving to the Vietnam Wall, I put on the turquoise necklace and look at my reflection in the passenger-side mirror.

"You really like that, don't you?" asks Dad.

"I love it," I say, trying to convey how much I really do.

"You know, Leah," he says, "if you want something from me, it's okay to just ask."

I'm quiet because sometimes that's true and sometimes it isn't.

We circle the area around the Wall looking unsuccessfully for a parking spot. Finally, Dad drives away from the crowds and into a more industrial part of the city filled mostly with office buildings emptied for the night. He tells me how DC is really two cities—the part the tourists come to see and the part with one of the highest murder rates in the country.

We park the car in front of a meter and walk toward the Wall, Dad's camera equipment knocking at his legs, though as usual he doesn't seem to notice. The sun has set but it isn't yet dark. Magic hour, Dad calls it. It's the light in which he wants to photograph the Vietnam Memorial, so we trudge past the Lincoln Memorial.

"Should we climb the stairs?" I ask.

Dad surveys the steps, holding out the front of his damp shirt, his face flushed in the heat. "I think it will be there for a while," he says.

"It's so *hot*," I say.

"Almost there," Dad says. "I promise it's worth it."

When we get to the Vietnam Memorial and descend the angled walkway running parallel to its marble wall, I understood what he means. As we move down the side of the Wall, a hush falls across the area. I reach out and touch the cool polished stone, then, realizing what I'm doing, I pull my hand away.

"It's okay," says Dad. "It's what you're supposed to do. It's designed that way."

All around us are large men, many of them in leather vests, tattoos running down their arms. One man with a long gray ponytail traces a name onto a piece of paper and weeps. A man in a suit stands a bit back from the crowd. He looks as if he has just stopped by the monument on his way home from work. Tears spill down his face from behind his sunglasses.

Dad takes photos of the adjacent monument, a statue of three infantrymen looking into the middle distance. He tells me the story of Maya Lin who won the contest to design the Wall and the ensuing fury. How they'd hired a well-known sculptor to create this other statue because they didn't know if people would "get" Lin's vision.

"Plus," says Dad, "she was an Asian woman. But you can see which monument matters more." We look toward the marble wall, all the people gathered there.

"Is it an anniversary or something?" I ask.

"Leah," he says, "I've been here maybe a dozen times. And I've never not seen a grown man crying his eyes out. Big tough guys. Sobbing. It never stops being real for us. This place. It's really important." Dad shows me how the names are arranged in chronological order, and how to find a specific person by looking them up in the large tattered books stationed around the wall.

"People wanted the names in alphabetical order, but Maya Lin pointed out you would wind up with, like, twenty-five Kevin Carrolls all in a line. The whole point was that this was personal. It wasn't that." He turns around and points at the statue of the infantrymen. "But in this light. What a gorgeous shot that will be."

I watch Dad think about his shot, about the way the light will play off the intricately molded faces. It's sad here, but it's a kind of soaring sadness, and I don't mind just standing, taking it all in.

When we leave, it's dark, and we walk through the deserted city center back to the car. Dad walks briskly in front of me, his tripod slung over his shoulder, navigating the city streets. I almost bump into him when he stops in front of a homeless man who leans against a building, panhandling.

"Anything you got, man," he says and folds his cardboard sign to hold out his hand. Dad puts his tripod down and digs through his pockets. Usually, they're full of change, piles of it that he pulls out by the fistful and drops into a large vase at the end of the day. And he always gives change to people asking for it on the street. Sometimes, walking through Providence or Boston, we'll get stopped two and three times and Dad will plunk a fistful of change into an outstretched palm.

Now, with Dad looking down, the man stares at the side of his face and wrinkles his forehead. "Kevin?"

Dad looks up. The two men look each other in the eye for a long silent beat.

"Hey man," says Dad, holding out his hand. The homeless man slides his hand against his palm, and they lock fingers for a moment before letting go. Dad peels two twenties from the stack of bills in his pocket.

"Thanks, Kev," says the man and turns to look at me as if he has just noticed I'm there. Dad has started walking away.

"Who was that?" I ask.

"Some guy I was in Vietnam with," he says.

"Seriously?" I ask. It seems too staged, too unreal.

Dad opens the trunk and throws in his tripod and camera bag, saying nothing. I get into the passenger seat and Dad starts the car, puts it into first gear. He looks over his shoulder to be sure it's clear and says, finally, "There but for the grace of God, go I."

I have nothing to say in response. I've forgotten what it can be like to be with Dad for more than just a couple of hours at a time, the way the universe seems to line up for him in a more dramatic way than it does for the rest of us.

We drive home the next day, stopping in Baltimore to see the Edgar Allan Poe house. Driving down the streets lined with row houses is like nothing I've ever seen before. In the abusive heat, everyone stands on their porches or out in the street. Someone has pried open a fire hydrant and children jump through the pulsing water. I didn't realize that even happened outside the movies. This is a larger collection of black people than I have ever seen in my life. I say that to Dad and he laughs.

"Rhode Island, you know," he starts, and then is quiet for a moment considering what he wants to say. "Some places it's really easy to be open-minded. It can be really easy to talk about equality when you go to the Stop and Shop, and it's filled with other white people."

We're driving around, trying to find the Poe house, the windows rolled up and the air-conditioning pumping. Dad says, "We'll just have to ask someone," and before I protest he rolls down my window and I'm staring up at a tall black woman in a bright-pink tank top.

"Um," I say.

The woman rolls her eyes and before I can even ask, she says, "Poe house is that way. Down this street, take a right."

When we get there, we're surprised to see that the house is in the middle of a residential block, a narrow row house just like the others, except that this one has a sign affixed to the door. It's closed because of the heat. Unsafe conditions.

"What about all the people who live in the houses around here?" I ask.

Instead we go to Poe's grave in a tiny church cemetery surrounded on all sides by busy city streets. Cars roll past, the windows down and music pouring from them into the thick air.

"Look," I say to Dad, showing him the dates on Poe's grave. "He died on October seventh. My birthday." I'm sure it means something. Dad smiles at me in a way that's so rare, I practically glow when it happens. I'm sure he doesn't realize it looks different, but it does; it's slower, less self-aware. I never know what I've done to deserve it.

ELEVEN

———•———

It takes a while to sink in that I'm not headed for college. I suppose I'd thought all along that somewhere along the line my inherent genius would be acknowledged despite the fact that the only classes I'd made passing grades in during my junior year were health and ceramics. I'd talked to Dad on the car ride home from Washington, DC, about maybe going to the New England School of Photography. It's your portfolio that counts there, not your grades. But we never follow up and when school starts in September, my guidance counselor calls me into her office.

"You realize you don't have enough credits to graduate, right?" she asks me. "I think you are probably a smart girl, Leah. What will you do?"

I look down at my hands folded in the lap of my corduroy skirt. Why is she asking me? I have no idea what you do if it's not getting up most days for high school. I have no idea what the next step is.

"That outfit!" says the guidance counselor. "See how creative you are? Did you make it yourself? Let me see up close!"

I lift my foot so she can see where I've cut off the ruffled hem of an old nightgown and sewn it into the bottom of the skirt.

"Have you ever thought of being a fashion designer?"

I blushed and roll my eyes. I've never thought of being a fashion designer. I love making clothes and coming up with the patterns in my head but as much as I protest otherwise, if I had money to go to the mall, that is where I would have bought my clothes instead. I leave the office finally understanding that there is no way I will graduate from high school that year. I can either take a fifth year or get my GED. I shudder at the thought of a fifth year, a second-year senior. It means disrupting the natural order of things. Four years and then college. That's how it works.

I keep the information to myself and don't do anything about it. I still get up most days and go to school, though more and more I have Ann-Marie call in sick for me. I write long poems during science class, sneak out for iced coffee during my remedial accounting class, and stare blankly out the window during European history, snapping to attention only as everyone begins gathering their backpacks and moving on to the next class.

My relationship with Ann-Marie is not going well. She's

started dating a man who owns a fashionable salon in Barrington, and is smitten. With his children grown, he has little interest in befriending her two sullen teenagers, one of them an accident of marriage. One night while Ann-Marie is at her boyfriend's, I'm watching Taylor, and she tells me in her tiny doll voice all the things she has done with her mom and her mom's new boyfriend and how she hopes that he might be her daddy one day.

"You have a daddy," I tell her. I'm perched on the edge of the tub, filling the rust-stained porcelain with warm water for Taylor's bath. "And he loves you very much."

Taylor balances herself and gingerly lifts a chubby leg over the side and into the water. Once she's situated herself in a pile of bubbles she looks up at me. "Mommy says that Daddy loves me very much. But that he is very sick."

The last time my dad had taken Taylor out alone she'd come home with a Barbie car he'd clearly managed to rip the security tag off and walk off without paying for. Ann-Marie was furious and I wondered if it was the first time she knew that Dad shoplifted. I'd seen him do it hundreds of times, even when they were still married. He'd pay for a basket full of groceries and then slide a box of razors into his pants while the clerk counted his money.

"Daddy's not sick," I say.

"Mommy says that Daddy is sick in his brain and his heart." When I don't say anything she continues. "Mommy says that you and Derek are lazy, too. Mommy says I am the best girl."

I splash water at Taylor and try to smile. "I don't want to hear anything else Mommy said, okay?"

———◆———

IN DECEMBER, OUR increasing tension explodes in a huge argument in the kitchen of the apartment. We lob insults back and forth at each other until finally I sneer, "Well at least I'm not a slut." Ann-Marie goes from angry to furious, chasing me into the corner between the refrigerator and the front door, smacking at me with both palms as I hold my hands over my head.

"I'm calling your father," she screams after me as I run into my bedroom and shut the door. "If you don't appreciate me you can go live with him."

Dad pulls up in front of the house a few hours later. I shiver inside my patchy faux-fur coat and wait in his car while he and Ann-Marie talk on the front porch. He walks down the steps, gets into the car, starts the engine, and sighs deeply. "Are you hungry?" he asks.

We eat at Caserta's Pizza near his apartment. We order our pizza and as we sit down in one of the orange booths waiting for our number to be called, Dad pours a bottle of Miller Lite into a plastic cup. "If this is going to work," he says, "we'll have to be more honest with each other. So I'm going to have a beer. And you're not going to freak out."

For so many years Dad has done his drinking sneakily. He has always preferred to drink in bars where he is the life of the party, the regular everyone loves. But as time went on he'd started drinking surreptitiously in the house, sneaking sips of whiskey from hidden bottles. I don't think I've seen him casually drink a beer since I was a child. But I promise him I won't freak out.

"If what's going to work out?" I ask.

Dad wipes foam from his mustache. I notice that the silver of his beard looks almost yellow in some places. "If we're going to live together," he says. "You really fucked up this time, you know. She doesn't want you back."

For all of my problems with Ann-Marie I can't imagine leaving Barrington, and I never thought she would kick me out for good. I launch into a tirade about how selfish she is, about how all she cares about is her stupid hairdresser boyfriend, about how she says mean things about me to Taylor. By the time I'm done, our pizza is ready and Dad carries it to the table.

"She's a good woman. I really wanted to love her," he says. "But in the end I think I married her so you could have a mom. I thought if I married her you'd have a normal family. Didn't work out so well, I guess."

When we get to Dad's apartment it's past eleven and I'm exhausted. He lives on the fourth floor of an old Victorian house in a one-bedroom with sloped ceilings and a kitchen alcove. The space itself had been renovated fairly recently with nice gray carpet and fresh white paint. It's furnished with the remnants of our small house on Carpenter Avenue—the white leather love seat that matches the sofa Ann-Marie had taken to the apartment, the brass headboard from their old bedroom, the glass coffee table that had sat in the upstairs living room after the basement of our old house was furnished. It's tidy but smells off, as if it has never been scrubbed. The coffee table is covered in sticky ringlets from bottles and glasses, and Dad's gray hairs cling to every surface in the bathroom.

"The futon is pretty comfortable," says Dad. "I fall asleep out here a lot of nights." He gives me a pillow and the comforter from his bed and shows me how his remote control works and then goes in his room and shuts the door. Within minutes, I hear him snoring. I lie awake in front of the TV watching a marathon of *Mystery Science Theater 3000*. Finally at two a.m., still awake, I turn on the light and wander around the apartment.

Dad has some paper plates in his cabinet and a bottle of Jameson. The silverware drawer is stuffed with the little plastic packets of soy sauce and spicy mustard from the Chinese restaurant. There's a lemon in the fridge and some more moldering condiments. On the wall by the front door a brand-new mountain bike is suspended by two hooks. I can't imagine Dad riding through the city on it and it doesn't look as if it has ever been used. He'd used the stationary bike all the time back at home, but this fancy chrome-and-fluorescent thing seems like an impulse purchase that didn't pan out. I scan the books in his small bookcase, pulling out Kay Redfield Jamison's *Touched with Fire*, and curl up under the comforter with it, falling asleep after a few pages detailing Sylvia Plath's madness and urge to create. I prefer Anne Sexton's poetry, but Plath's mental illness feels so much more urgent and real. I wonder if she might be my favorite poet after all.

Over the next week Dad and I develop a routine. We go to the coffee shop in Providence where he has recently taken me for my first espresso, and we buy cappuccinos, drinking them as he drives me to school in the mornings. I feel very sophisticated. At night I take the city bus into Providence and Dad picks me up on Thayer Street. We eat pizza and Thai food. We eat Chinese from the restaurant around the corner where Dad places all his orders under the name Mr. White, an homage to the character from *Reservoir Dogs*, and where the woman who rings us up laughs and points at his hair. "Mr. White!" she says.

One night Dad takes me into a small green bar, like the ones he'd taken me to as a kid, called Blake's. He promises the burgers are the best. When we walk in everyone swivels around and greets him, clapping him on the back. Dad acknowledges them all with a nod and walks silently back to a corner table. I notice that he leaves most of his food on the plate every time we eat.

He talks about looking for a two-bedroom apartment so that I can have a room. We talk some more about going to school for photography. I don't tell him about my conversation with the guidance counselor. There are moments when I think maybe it can work, when I wonder why I'd gone with Ann-Marie in the first place, like the afternoon we speed around Providence from one florist shop to another trying to find a perfect red rose to photograph before we lose the light of sunset. But there are other moments, like the time he doesn't pick me up from Thayer Street, and I have to make my way through the unfamiliar streets of Providence to his house, that I feel sick with dread. When I finally get there I find him asleep on the couch, the TV muted. He stares at me in the doorway, his eyes blank.

"I'm starving," I tell him. "Can we order a pizza?"

"Jesus Christ, Leah," he says. "I can't afford for us to eat out every fucking night, you know."

That night, playing around with the remote control, I accidentally eject a video from the VCR. It's a porno called *Summer Camp Sluts*.

A few nights later Dad picks me up and drops me off in front of his building telling me he'll be back later on. I watch TV and talk on the phone to Alex, telling her how much I'm dying for a cigarette even though I'm not really. I go on the computer in Dad's room, dialing up his modem to connect to the Internet, but I can't find anything interesting to read. I don't really get what's so exciting about the whole Internet thing. Unless you know what site you want to get to it's mostly just the same thing over and over. I won't have an email account for another two years. Finally, I turn off the light and watch TV in the darkness. I turn the volume up loud enough so I can't hear the rush of cars on the highway near the apartment. The sound unnerves me.

From downstairs there's a large bang. I jump up terrified, thinking someone has broken into the house. Then I hear Dad calling my name. I freeze, too afraid of what I might see if I open the door, but he keeps calling for me and I'm afraid the neighbors will come out or call the police on him. I walk out onto the back stairway.

"Dad?" I call.

"Leah," he says. "Leah, Leah…" I walk down a flight of stairs and find him sprawled across the landing. He has a gash on his forehead and has peed his pants. I'm sure everyone in the building will be able to smell the urine and whiskey emanating from his body in waves, and I want to save him from the embarrassment, but I stand there, afraid to get any closer.

"Leah," he says, "I need your help."

Panicked again that somebody might call the police on us, I reach out my hand. He grabs it and, trying to pull himself up, all six foot two and two hundred pounds of him, he pulls me down instead. I fall hard on my knee on the landing, missing two steps.

"Dad!" I hiss. "Dad, get the fuck up. Get up!" I don't know where it comes from. I've never talked to him like that. Something about it registers with him too, because he hauls himself into a standing position and sways back and forth up the stairs. I stand behind him trying to make sure that he doesn't fall, and that I don't get crushed if he does. When we get into the apartment he walks into his room and throws himself down on the bed. I go to the opposite side of the apartment, underneath the suspended mountain bike, and sit in the corner trying to figure out what to do. Should I leave? Should I make sure his head is okay?

Then he calls my name again. I ignore it, sure he will just pass out if I sit there long enough and make myself small enough in the corner. But he doesn't stop.

"Leah," he yells, "come in here."

I stand up and yell back. "No," I say. "I'm not coming in there. Go to sleep." I pace around the kitchen, looking out the casement windows, absolutely unsure of what to do. I can't call Ann-Marie. I can't retreat to my room. I think about locking myself in the bathroom. Dad yells for me again. "Leah," he says. "I'm your dad." His voice breaks and he sobs like a child.

I put on my fake-fur coat, grab my backpack, and flee out the front door. Outside the night has turned frigid and I don't have gloves or a hat. I run down Atwells Avenue trying to keep from crying, so I can look tough on the city streets. In front of me are the blinking triple X's of the Columbus Theatre. I know from there it isn't far to Kennedy Plaza, the bus depot. I'm not sure what I will do when I get there but I know I can never, ever go back to Dad's apartment. I take the bus to Barrington and when I get there I call Reba from a pay phone. She and her mom pick me up at the bus stop in their blue mini van. We're silent during the short drive to Reba's house. I try to stifle tears and I can tell they feel embarrassed for me. Reba gets out the passenger-side door, and when it closes her mom turns to me and says, "You can stay here as long as you need to."

———◆———

REBA IS DOING her senior year at Phillips Exeter, which means that I can stay in her big drafty room while she's away in New Hampshire after the winter break ends. Her family has books lining the walls and strewn over every surface. I try mostly to stay out of their way and read constantly. I read an illustrated biography of Frida Kahlo, marveling at her life and her vivid paintings. I read *The Great Gatsby* and *Jane Eyre*. I read *The Virgin Suicides* because I'm intrigued by the name and cover, and am blown away by its style and voice.

Reba's little sister is in Israel so I have the top floor—two bedrooms and a little bathroom with a stand-up shower—to myself. I creep quietly into Reba's sister's room and help myself to the clothes that hang there. I tell myself it's fine if I wear them just once and then hang them back up. But soon I've raided nearly all of her closet, filled with things from the mall that I'd never have been able to make or afford.

When Reba comes home one weekend she confronts me about it. "My mom says you're stealing Debbie's clothes." I'm mortified, both because it's true, and because I thought I had been getting away with it. I wonder how long her mom had noticed without saying anything, and how strange I must have seemed skulking around upstairs walking between bedrooms on the ancient squeaking hardwood floors. My thievery combined with the fact that at Reba's house I have a curfew causes me to slink back to Ann-Marie. She takes me back. She doesn't ask what happened at Dad's house, and I don't tell her.

Back in the apartment in Barrington, I fret endlessly about what will happen when high school is over and everyone leaves. One day, driving around in Alex's car, another friend tells me that his mother, who works in a bank, had come across an account in my name, but couldn't tell him anything more about it. She'd asked him to mention it to me. We drive to his house, where his mom tells me there is a trust fund set up in my name by the Rhode Island victims defense fund. If that's the case, and I have a little money, I can get emancipated. What would happen next, I'm not sure. Maybe I'll get a job at the library. Or at a fancy coffee shop like the one Dad took me to in Providence. The next morning I ask Ann-Marie about the trust fund. She's at the table eating a buttered English muffin and sipping from a lipstick-stained mug of coffee.

"Well you *did* have a trust fund," she says. "But you don't anymore. Your grandparents sued the state after the whole thing with your mom. That's where the money came from."

"Where is it now?" I ask.

"It went to pay off your dad's credit cards."

I know that Dad has hundreds of thousands of dollars in credit card debt. He buys compulsively, things like that mountain bike, with no intention of ever paying it back.

"How much was it for?" I ask.

Ann-Marie puts down her coffee mug. "It was for ten thousand dollars, but it doesn't really matter now because there is none of it left."

I'm shocked. Ten thousand dollars seems like an impossible amount of money to me. Enough I'm sure, to get my own apartment. Enough to buy a car for when Alex is in college and can no longer drive me around.

"I'm not going to graduate," I blurt out.

"So what are you going to do?" She cups one hand beneath the table and sweeps some crumbs into it, sprinkling them onto her plate.

"I don't know," I say.

"Maybe you should call your Aunt Sandy," she says. "Maybe she and your grandma will help you. You can't stay here if you're not in school."

I still see my grandparents and my Aunt Sandy on holidays and speak to them on the phone, but I can't imagine how they will help me. I've been so distant from them the last few years. My purple hair and nose ring made them worried I was turning into someone like my mom. Someone who might get in trouble. I'm not able to explain to them that I really only want to look bad, not be bad. I want to be a famous poet someday and need to be sharp to accomplish that goal. Still, despite all the time that has gone by, when I call my aunt I'm only a few words into my explanation of the situation before she sorts it out.

"You'll live here," she says. "Grammy can help us out

LEAH CARROLL

with bills and stuff. You have to take the GED, I guess.
And you can go to community college. It's right up the
street."

I burst into hysterical, hiccuping tears.

I hadn't realized how much I've wanted someone to step
in and just make a decision for me.

Because I'm only seventeen, I have to wait for the rest
of my high school class to graduate before I can take the
GED. I'm ashamed and keep it secret, still showing up to
school but mostly just wandering the hallways once I'm
there. I'm terrified everything about me will be exposed
if I'm a high school dropout: I'm trash, an imposter in this
quaint little town. I take and pass the GED in time for the
fall semester of 1998. I'll be seventeen, turning eighteen
that October.

That summer I move in with my aunt, uncle, and my
sweet, hyperactive nine-year-old cousin. As much as I'd
whined about having to babysit Taylor, I miss her like
crazy. When I see a little girl on TV my heart aches. I apply
for jobs all over the place and waiting to hear back I stay
out all day on the back porch. I swim short, circular laps in
the above-ground pool and read books from the Cranston
Public Library.

In the evenings Alex or Reba drive from Barrington to
Cranston to pick me up. We know a boy whose parents
have taken an extended vacation and left him in charge
of the enormous house perched on the edge of the bay. A
group of us take it over, sleeping on the couches and in his

parents' bedroom and sometimes on the back lawn by the water. We trip on mushrooms and drink grappa pilfered from the liquor cabinet out of juice glasses and talk about where we will all be in the fall. I spend long sweltering nights in a spare attic bedroom, a giant box fan propped up by the twin bed. Late at night, with no TV to distract me, and not wanting to wake anyone else in the house, I think about Dad and about my mom, and where my life is going and if I have any control over it at all.

I call Dad for the first time since my stay with him in the winter to let him know I've gotten my GED. "I've got something I want to give you," he says. We arrange for him to come by Aunty Sandy's house. I hang his photos around the little basement room I have at my aunt's. Anytime I hear about a drunk driving accident, on the news or in the paper, I pay special attention, worried it's him.

When Dad pulls into the driveway I go outside to meet him. He wears shorts and tennis shoes without socks and his ankles are red and swollen over the side of the sneakers. He carries his large camera bag and his tripod.

"Here," he says. "I want you to have these." He rolls the tripod onto the grass and lifts the bag off his shoulder.

"What does that mean?" I ask. I interpret his gesture as a way to make me feel guilty for having spurned him. It's like he wants me to think he's giving me all the stuff that matters to him most because he won't be around for long. I hate that he manipulates me so easily. I try to tell myself it isn't my fault he is alone now. But inside I don't really believe it. He's my dad. I think of being small and riding on his shoulders through the grocery store. I think of being sick and how he'd hold my hair back while I vomited. I'd seen him at his worst and abandoned him. But I can't make any of these thoughts into words.

"Nothing. I'm just going to be leaving for a while. I thought you'd want this stuff."

Though leaving is something he's threatened to do before—to Boston to work for the *Globe*, to Florida to go in with a buddy on a restaurant he's starting—I still panic a little when he says it. What if I really never see him again? But somehow I worry more that he might *not* leave. That he'll stay in Rhode Island and eventually I'll have to go back to that apartment and when I get there he'll be bleeding, or sick, or worse.

"What did he want?" asks my aunt once he's driven away.

"He said he's going away and he doesn't need this stuff," I say, lugging the heavy bag filled with lenses and filters and flashes into the house.

"What does that mean?" she asks.

"He said he got offered a job at the *Globe*, you know. He might take it," I lie.

———

THAT FALL I begin classes at the Community College of Rhode Island. I cash in ten years' worth of premature savings bonds Ann-Marie's parents have been giving me for my birthdays since childhood. A friend is driving across the country in a van, and so I pay her three hundred dollars for her 1987 Ford Escort. I'm obsessed with the car. It has vinyl seats and bald tires and no radio. I put a boom box in the passenger side and perfect my stick shift, driving around for hours singing at the top of my lungs.

With the Escort, I have freedom. I can go wherever I want, whenever I want. The only real problem is that I don't have anywhere to go. For the first time that I can remember I'm so lonely that it feels like I exist in a deep, dark spreading shadow. I miss Taylor. I miss my dad, whom I can almost never get on the phone and whom I'm worried about even more since he gave me his camera stuff. When I do get him, we only talk for just a few minutes before one of us makes an excuse to hang up.

One night, driving around aimlessly, I decide to visit Dad at the bar. When I walk in he's involved in what looks like a deep conversation with another patron, a man who looks remarkably like him. I tap him on the shoulder and register the surprise in his eyes when he sees me.

"Leah, this is Billy Temple," he says as he stands up. "Billy, this is my daughter." The man shakes my hand and smiles, like he knows me.

I tell Dad about my car and we go out to the parking lot to have a look. Downtown Providence on a weekday night is ghostly quiet. The brick buildings around the lot still bear the fading painted signs of the factories and department stores they had once been. Someone nearby, but out of sight, smashes a glass bottle and the sound echoes.

"Five-speed?" asks Dad.

"Of course," I say.

"I taught you well," he says, then squeezes my shoulder lightly and walks back into the bar.

A few weeks later I try calling his apartment and find the number is disconnected. For the next three nights I call and call, getting the same operator's message each time. Finally I call the bar.

"He's not in tonight," says the bartender. I think I might have to explain what he looks like, but as soon as I say Kevin Carroll the man knows who I'm talking about. "But he was here last night. Have you tried Murphy's?" I don't call Murphy's. It's enough to know they've seen him recently.

In my composition class at the Community College of Rhode Island, I write a free-write exercise about my dad. I write about how he was a Vietnam vet and the smartest person I know, but that sometimes I hate him. The teacher, a bearded, wild-haired man who insists we call him by his first name, Bob, hands back the papers, and then as everyone shuffles out of the room, he calls my name.

"Your dad's name isn't Kevin, is it?" he asks.

"It is," I say. "How did you know?"

"Your paper," he says. "I used to work at the *Journal*. Still write for them sometimes. I read about a scary-smart guy, Vietnam vet, then saw your last name. Your dad is one of a kind. I was pretty sure it was him. So he's not doing that great, I take it?"

"Not really," I say, embarrassed. I hadn't expected to have to discuss the paper, much less be found out.

"You tell your dad that Bob says hi. And that his daughter is just as talented and smart as he is." Bob gathers his tattered sheaf of papers and leaves. I stay behind in the classroom, reading and rereading my essay.

❖

FOR CHRISTMAS THAT year, I buy Derek a pair of Patriots sweatpants, and Taylor, who is four years old, a Teletubby doll. I buy a paperback edition of *A Long Day's Journey into Night* for Dad. I'd wanted to get him *The Iceman Cometh* because it's his favorite play, but they don't stock it in the Warwick Mall Waldenbooks. He'd taken me the year before to a small production of *Hamlet*, and I was mesmerized by the way the words came alive in a way they never had during high school English class.

The day after Christmas, Dad calls me at my aunt's.

"You sound so shocked," he says. "I am your dad."

We meet for lunch at Murphy's. Dad orders French onion soup and the cheese hangs from strings in his mustache as he eats. I hand him a napkin. We eat our sandwiches and pickles and I tell him about Bob. He laughs.

I start to talk about Taylor, to tell him about everything she has gotten for Christmas and that I really miss not living with her. Dad stops me.

"I really can't talk about Taylor right now," he says.

The waitress comes by to see if we want more coffee. I think about it for a second, looking at my watch.

"Have another cup," says Dad. We drink another cup of coffee and talk about *Schindler's List,* which I've just seen. Dad talks about the Liam Neeson character, how amazingly he has been rendered. He catches my eye for a moment and we both look away.

"I should get going," I say.

"I'll walk you to your car," he says.

We walk down Fountain Street, near the *Journal* offices, to the lot where I've parked the Escort.

"I had a really fun time in Washington, DC," I say. It comes out of nowhere, but it seems important to say.

"I did too," Dad says. He crumples his chin the way he does when he's thinking hard about something. "I had a really good time."

I stand by the door of the Escort. I feel like I should hug Dad good-bye. I can't get in touch with him and I don't know when I will see him again. But I can't make myself put my arms around him. It's like there's an invisible barrier, years of so much unsaid, blocking the way between us.

"Okay," I say, getting into the car. He waves good-bye as I reverse the car out of its spot.

Two days later he's dead.

TWELVE

———◆———

When I walk into the door of my Aunt Sandy's house she's sitting on the corner of the couch, shaking her leg frantically. I can see the panic in her eyes and know right away what she's going to say.

"Hold on one second," I say. I walk back out the door and rummage through my purse, my heart pounding. I think maybe I can just not go back in. If I don't go back in none of this will happen. My aunt comes out and meets me out on the step.

"It's your dad, Leah," she says. "He died."

"Okay," I say, nodding in confirmation. I walk to the kitchen table, hang my coat over one of the chairs, and put my bag down. "Okay, okay, okay." I'm nodding and nodding, my head bobbing up and down. My aunt stands next to me, holding my arm.

"Leah?"

My knees wobble, and suddenly I'm on the ground, howling. I keep thinking about the hug. I keep thinking about how he'd asked me to stay for one more cup of coffee. I've thought all those years it had been wrong of him to never tell me directly about my mom's death and how he'd abandoned me as much as I abandoned him. But I realize at that moment that what he'd been trying to do was spare me just this exact feeling. This knowledge that no matter what, he's never ever coming back. The knowledge that I'll never get to atone for abandoning him.

———

AUNT RITA'S SON convinces the obituary section writer of the *Journal* to list his place of death as Aunt Rita's house and not the Sportsman's Inn, the flophouse with a strip club on the first floor where he'd been staying off and on for the last couple of months. He'd burned through his severance and 401(k). I had worried what he'd do when he spent all that money, where he'd live. Now I know.

The details about his death are sketchy. There are whispers that when the manager at the Sportsman's found his body the call that went out to police dispatch was that there had been a suicide. But nobody can confirm that. His body is autopsied and then taken to the funeral parlor.

"I think you should go and see him one last time," Aunty Rita says to me. It has been years and years since we've spoken, but now suddenly she's back in my life. At the last moment I decide to go into the room and see his body. The funeral director tells me what to expect.

"He doesn't have any makeup or anything on. And we did a good job of cleaning it up, but you'll see there's a cut on the side of his head." He hands me a plastic bag.

"Everything he had with him should be in there. I have his clothes too, when you're done," he says. "Everything except his pants." The man looks flustered all of the sudden. "His pants were, they were . . . soiled."

He leads me into the room where Dad's body is on a kind of pedestal, a white sheet pulled up to his neck. He's going to be cremated, a desire he'd expressed to me and Ann-Marie over and over again, so there's no coffin. I walk up to him, looking down at his face. It has gone a bit sunken already, but there's his silver hair, his mustache. It's him. I lean forward and kiss him on the forehead, touching him for the first time in years. His skin is very, very cold and I feel aware of the way it stretches over his bones, holding his insides together like a package. *There's nobody in there*, I think.

Aunty Rita decides on a Catholic Mass for Dad, though he'd converted to Judaism to marry my mother and had discussed his disgust for all religions on more occasions than I can possibly count. I think maybe he might see the humor in these priests waving around their incense and holy water over a heathen. And a Jewish one at that.

At the Mass, my cousin Shawn, Rita's son who's in his

late twenties, talks about how his uncle was the coolest
guy he knew, how because of him Shawn had the coolest sneakers when he was a teenager. He cries the whole
time and struggles to get through a reading of Dylan
Thomas:

Do not go gentle into that good night,
Old age should burn and rave at close of day;
Rage, rage against the dying of the light.

In the receiving line, I shake endless hands. There are a
lot of men my dad's age who are crying. The incongruity of
it reminds me of being at the Vietnam Memorial. After the
Mass I'm invited to Blake's for the Irish wake they're holding in his honor. There are more crying men there, telling
me how much my dad meant to them. I drink Heineken
and shots of Jameson in his honor. I feel special and I feel
guilty for feeling special.

"To Kevin," someone will yell, and then everyone echoes
"To Kevin!" and then we all swallow our whiskey. I vomit
in the bar bathroom but I haven't eaten all day or the day
before and there's nothing in my stomach except for some
sour bile that dribbles reluctantly out of my body. One of
the young waitresses rubs my back and tells me how she'd
thought of Dad as a kind of father, too, how warm and nur-
turing he was, and how he respected all the girls, and she
just felt safe with him. I heave over the toilet bowl, feeling

like something in my digestive system will rip open if it doesn't stop soon—because that's not how I feel about him at all.

I drive home on 95 with my little boom box off, still half drunk and trying hard to focus on the lines in the road. Suddenly there's a high screeching noise all around me. I think something is caught in my tires and pull off to the shoulder, coming to a stop. But the sound doesn't go away. Then I realize it's me. I'm shrieking. Even after I realize, I can't stop. It feels like I might sit there all night screaming and digging my nails deep into my skin.

———————

DAD'S BODY IS cremated and the death certificate we need to give to a seemingly endless number of people—my school, his bank (where his remaining two hundred dollars is in a checking account), the tow lot where his Jetta was stashed, the storage facility where all his stuff had been taken when he'd been evicted, months before—lists his cause of death as natural, the result of an exploded heart and used-up liver. When we get the official report with his cause of death, the police officer who owns Blake's hands me a small square of paper. He tells me he wasn't able to give it to me until after the autopsy results. It's a suicide note. I don't know what else to call it. Apparently he'd gone to a friend's house, typed it on her computer, and asked the bartender at Blake's to hold it for me. Initially, the bartender refused—he was not going to let Kevin go out like that—but he put it aside for safekeeping when my dad left the note behind on the bar.

Unfolding the paper and reading his words, almost a month after seeing his dead body and burying his ashes in the Carroll family plot next to his beloved mother and despised father, is like hearing him speak again. He wrote:

> Leah, try to understand this is not your fault. I'm not mad at anyone or trying to punish anyone. I just can't live inside my own head anymore. Depression and alcoholism have ruined my life.
>
> The proudest moment of my life was when you were six and read the Night Before Christmas at Ann-Marie's mother's house on the Eve. I'm proud of you now by going to school and doing something interesting with your life.
>
> I always loved you more than life even if I couldn't show it to you most of the time.
>
> Try to see Beethoven's Ninth with the chorale in person sometime. It's magical.
>
> Read the Mark Twain short story the Five Boons of Life to try to understand how I feel.
>
> Take lots of pictures.
>
> Use my car, the exhaust is new, it should last a long time

I love you take care of Taylor let her know I
wasn't that bad a guy
Use your mind

————•————

AFTER DAD DIES, I'm worried I will wind up like my
parents and also terrified that I might not. By the time
I finally make it to a four-year college in 2001, I've rein-
vented myself as wholesome, and capable, a possessor of
material things that prove my worth: hundreds of books,
monogrammed handbags, cashmere twin sets, and pearl
earrings. I'm meticulous about my appearance. Each night
I flat iron my thick, frizzy hair into a gleaming mane and in
the mornings I wrap my ponytail in a pastel ribbon.

My friends and I hang out in a decrepit bar on Boylston
street near our campus in Boston. We're writing students pretending to be writers. We drink our afternoons
away discussing David Foster Wallace and one upping
each other with obscure pop-culture trivia. With enough
foamy beer in me I feel warm and confident. Surrounded
mostly by boys, I assert myself loudly and bombastically.
I can swear, quote Joyce, rap every lyric to "Juicy," and
frost a layer cake. My headbands and my penny loafers are
my armor. I want to be the girl who gets drunk with the
boys at two p.m. on a Tuesday and also the girl who young
mothers ask to hold their toddler's hand outside of a public
restroom.

I go into my college computer lab, access the *Providence Journal* archives, and type in my mother's name. The articles are behind a paywall, and I have to pay to access them. I punch in my debit card number and read everything Dean Starkman had written. It seems so strange that I can read those words, "Give us the death rattle," and all around me people work on papers and check Friendster and have no idea what is happening. I have the Yeats line in my head: the lonely impulse of delight. I log off the computer, grab my bag, and walk to the bar where my friends are drinking and laughing in the gloom.

"Let's get shots!" I say. When I get my wallet out to pay, I discover it's gone. I run back to the computer lab where I find my wallet next to the computer I'd been using. Somebody has taken all the cash but left everything else behind.

———•———

YEARS LATER, I sit at another funeral, this time surrounded by the Rhode Island Chapter of the Combat Veterans Motorcycle Association, and think of the last time I had seen the man in the coffin, Billy Temple: my dad's best friend in his final years. The vets stand at attention around the edges of the room. They're stone-faced and turned out in leather vests and American flags. Their tattoos mark their time in various wars, mostly Vietnam, but I notice one or two younger men, younger than me surely, with patches affixed to their leather jackets denoting their service in Iraq and Afghanistan.

I thought that surely I would see Billy Temple again, that I would get to ask him more questions about who my father was and what he was doing in the days before he died. I thought in some way that my dad's tragedy was singular to me and that it couldn't be duplicated or improved upon. But ten years after my father's death, Billy Temple, a former police officer who carried a concealed weapon, was involved in a minor car accident on Nooseneck Road in Coventry. When the police arrived, he turned the gun on one of the officers. I think that must have been the moment when, as a former police officer himself, he knew it was all over. Billy sat for a bit in the car, weapon pointed at his chin, then stepped out of the vehicle, moved the gun to the side of his head, and fired a single shot. By the time he was transported to Kent Hospital, the hospital where I had been born, he was dead.

The last time I saw Billy Temple alive, I'd been twenty-five and was collecting more information about my parents. I met him at Twin Oaks, an Italian restaurant in Cranston.

When I walked in, Billy turned on his bar stool, rose to meet me, and asked, "Can I get you a drink?" It was three o'clock in the afternoon, and the winter sun reflected off the Pawtuxet River, pouring into the oak-and-maroon interior of the lounge area where we sat.

"I'll have a glass of Pinot Grigio," I told him. The bartender, in his white shirt and black vest, looked at me. He reached for a wineglass and winked at Billy.

"This is Kevin Carroll's daughter," said Billy, and the bartender's whole face changed. I pretended not to notice, joking instead with Billy about my baby face and getting carded. Billy drank from a snifter of Grand Marnier, and I tried to keep it together next to this man who looked and acted so much like my dad. I took a big swallow of wine.

Earlier that day, before meeting Billy, I'd picked up my dad's autopsy report from the Rhode Island medical examiner's office. In the car I tore open the manila envelope stamped CONFIDENTIAL and read the disclaimer on the first sheet of paper.

This report provides an explicit description of the deceased's Injury(s),disease(s), or characteristic(s). When present, postmortem Changes brought about by natural decomposition after death and additional Postmortem artifacts are also described in the report(s).

Please consider that the report may have an adverse impact on the Reader. The reader may want the support of family, friends, clergy, or personal Physician during their review of the enclosed report. Regretfully, the emotional Effects of these reports cannot be predicted or prevented without sacrificing the legal and scientific value of the report itself.

I felt a sad and perverse little thrill go through me as I shuffled through the pages. It came from this proof of things, from the physicality of the fourteen-page autopsy report. In deciding to retrace my dad's last day alive, the office of the medical examiner was my first step.

The place was something straight out of central casting: basement level, concrete floors, and permed receptionists with thick Rhode Island accents. I introduced myself as the next of kin and they chewed gum and unlocked a filing cabinet. I wondered what it must be like to work in that basement office all day. I wondered if the women packed Tupperware containers of leftover pasta or if they went out on their lunch break for sandwiches. All of it gave me a strange sense of satisfaction. This was how things should be.

The first page of the report read:

The body is that of a normally developed, adequately nourished, adult white male who appears approximately the stated age 48 years. The measured height is 72 inches, and the scale weight is 225 pounds. Rigor mortis is present and equally developed in the extremities. Livor Mortis is light purple, posterior, dependent and fixed. The body is cold to touch. The scalp hair is gray, measuring up to 1 1/2 inches in length. A laceration to the right side of the head and superior portion of the right ear will be described under evidence of Injury. There are no palpable fractures. The external auditory canals are dry. The irises are hazel/blue. The pupils are round, symmetric and measure 0.5 cm in diameter. The cornea are clear. The conjunctivae and sclerae are unremarkable. The nose is palpably intact in the midline, and the left nostril contains a slight amount of grumous, dried, dark brown fluid, extending over the upper lip. The teeth are natural and in good repair. There is no evidence of injury to the lips, tongue or oral mucous membranes. The anterior structures of the neck are palpably intact in the midline. The neck veins are slightly distended, and there is upper chest, neck, and facial plethora. The chest cage is symmetric and intact with mildly increased anterior to posterior diameter. There is mild bilateral gynecomastia. The abdomen is firm and atraumatic. The lower extremities are symmetric and intact. The feet are clean and atraumatic. The upper extremities are symmetric and intact. The hands are clean and atraumatic and the fingernails are fairly well groomed. The thoracic, lumbar, and sacral spines are palpably intact. The anus is clean and atraumatic. There is no unusual or distinctive odor about the body.

When received the body is clothed in blue denim pants, a black leather belt, a black long sleeve sweater, a gray sock, and a "Timberland" brown boot the left boot and sock have been removed from the body for attachment of the toe tag.

There were so many items to linger over. So many famil-iar details that, when couched in the clinical language of the autopsy, took on a sinister sheen of wonder. My dad's blue eyes I'd always wished for in place of my own brown ones. The gray hair that stayed so thick and silver, even as the rest of his body descended into the stink and bloat of drinking. The secret and private areas of his body laid out beneath a cold, clinical glare: his nostrils, his anus, his neck veins.

The one Timberland boot triggered a memory of seeing his body at the funeral home. The funeral director hand-ing me those very boots in a plastic bag and saying, "I'm sorry we can't give you the pants..."

With this memory, I realized, because of those boots—because there were two of them in the bag—that when I saw my dad's body in the funeral home, he had already been autopsied. If I'd pulled away the sheet tucked beneath his chin I would have seen the Y-shaped incision.

The seventy-two inches mentioned at the beginning of the report struck me as well. For all my dad's mythmaking, for all his tall tales and broken promises, there were certain facts about him of which I was sure. My dad was six feet and two inches tall. Of that I had no doubt. The medical examiner was insisting to me here, in measured pace and language taken from a template, that I was wrong. He was only six feet tall, it said. Your father is two inches shorter than you believed, the report said to me.

SITTING IN THE bar, I asked Billy Temple if it was okay
to record our conversation. With his thick white hair, and
impeccably groomed beard and mustache, he was a commanding presence.

"How did you two meet?" I asked.

Billy considered the question, took a drink from his glass.

"We were both in Blake's Tavern one night," he said. "I
had on a baseball hat with my platoon number on it. Kevin
came over to me and we got to talking about Vietnam. I
was in the navy. I never once was on a boat that whole war,
though. Your dad, I don't know if you know, he drove a
minesweeper—a suicide truck they called it."

Billy stopped for a minute and shook his empty glass at
the bartender, signaling for another. "Your dad and I—" He
stopped again, a hitch in his throat. The bartender placed
a new glass of Grand Marnier on a cocktail napkin in front
of him and swept the empty away in one swift movement.
Billy swallowed. "Your dad and I, we were the same kind
of guy." He wiped at a tear and lifted his glass. "People are
gonna look over here and think you and me are breaking
up," he said. "Your dad was my best friend."

BLAKE'S TAVERN SITS at the corner of Mathewson and
Fountain Streets, two blocks from what was once the

Sportsman's Inn, the strip club and hotel where my dad died. It's now a boutique hotel called the Dean, and what was, while I was growing up, the blighted downcity of Providence seems more lively—there are more restaurants and nightclubs and reasons for people to be walking around. Still, in some ways the downcity section is an eerily vacant reminder of the industries that once supported the state and have since vanished. The crumbling facades of costume jewelry manufacturers and textile factories bear witness to an industrial past that once supported generations of Italian and Irish immigrants.

When Billy and my dad were regulars at Blake's it was owned by a former police lieutenant and populated by Providence's finest. The establishment, even then, was a relic within a relic. The walls were hung with pictures of the patrons and framed Irish blessings. The regulars clustered proprietarily around the left end of the large bar. After my dad died, someone nailed a small brass plaque to the wooden beam at one corner. It read: KEVIN CARROLL 1950–1998. I didn't know what to make of this. It looked to me like a grave marker, but to the regulars, the plaque was an elegy.

My dad's favorite story to tell about Blake's was the night that two hood rats came in scoping the bar for purses carelessly slung over stools. The owner approached the kids and ordered them to leave. One of them pulled a large knife and waved it menacingly at the former police lieutenant. Without missing a beat, he withdrew his large revolver from its holster and said, "Get the fuck out of my bar."

This was my dad's favorite part of the story. "It was like Crocodile Dundee!" he would say and laugh. "Like, you call that a knife? Now, this is a knife!"

———◆———

THE AUTOPSY REPORT concludes:

> It is my opinion that Kevin S. Carroll, a 48 year old white male, died as a result of cardiomegaly and steatosis of the liver associated with a clinical history of chronic ethanol use. Reportedly, the decedent had a longstanding history of heavy ethanol use and checked into a motel in an intoxicated state. When checked upon the following day, he was fully dressed with injuries to the right side of his head, consistent with a terminal collapse in a secure motel room. There was no evidence of bleeding throughout the room, supporting the fact that these injuries to the scalp were terminal events. At autopsy, he had an enlarged greasy liver with steatohepatitis, consistent with acute and chronic ethanol use, as well as an enlarged heart with microscopic findings consistent with hypertensive cardiovascular disease. An additional

significant contributing condition to his death included chronic obstructive pulmonary disease.

Cause of Death: Cardiomegaly and Steatosis of the Liver Associated with Clinical History of Chronic Ethanol Use. Other Significant Findings: Laceration to Scalp of Right Side of Head Due to Terminal Collapse and Chronic Obstructive Pulmonary Disease. Manner of Death: Natural.

———

I ASKED BILLY Temple if he knew about the note my dad had left me. Outside, the sun shone brilliantly over the water, and the light shifted in the bar. The bar began to come alive; people talking louder, their heads closer together. In the dining room there was the din of silverware against plates, and conversations began to rise in volume. A man in the entrance called out the names of parties to seat.

I nursed my glass of wine. Billy was on his third Grand Marnier. He said, "Your dad tried to give me that note. He told me that if anything ever happened to him I was supposed to give it to you. I told him I didn't want any part of it."

He stopped then to look at me. "What did the note say?" he asked.

I took a deep breath, because for quite a stretch in the bar, I'd been dry-eyed, but the note always reduced me to tears. I paraphrased for him, trying to keep my voice level. I didn't tell him, didn't need to tell him, that when the police detective gave it to me it felt like my heart turned completely inside out. It felt like I was hearing my dad speak again. It felt like I felt right then, sitting next to Billy Temple at the bar and hearing him tell stories.

Billy nodded slowly. "I said to him, 'I'm not gonna have anything to do with this. If you want to kill yourself, fine, but I'm not helping.' It got to the point where we were in the hallway at Blake's there and we were fighting, kind of pushing each other around. Your dad gave the note to Scotty, the bartender—do you remember him?" I nodded yes and Billy went on.

"Somehow we got outside. It was real cold, and you know how your dad dressed. Suit and tie all the time. But his shoes were untied, and his ankles, I could see they were all swollen. I said, 'Kev, when was the last time you went to a doctor, you asshole?'"

Billy laughed a little and pushed away his empty drink. "And I'm sorry to say—" He stopped, reached for the empty glass, looked at it and put it down again. "I'm sorry to say that our last words to each other were, your dad says to me, 'Fuck you, Billy Temple,' and I said, 'Fuck you right back, Kevin Carroll.'"

I wiped away tears, sniffed into a cocktail napkin. The bartender deposited a new drink in front of us and Billy picked it up. My phone had been ringing in my purse and I did my best to ignore it. Billy Temple began to look uncomfortable, as if he suspected that if he didn't say something, I might stay there all night with him.

"You got dropped off," he said. "You have a ride home, right?"

I blushed and dug the phone out of my bag.

"I do," I said, looking at my phone for the time. "I didn't realize how late it was getting. I have to go anyway." I pressed the SEND button to dial my ride.

Suddenly things were weird between Billy and me, in the way that things can get weird in a bar, after a certain number of drinks, after a certain hour of the day. He said, "If you want some dinner or something...Do you want something to eat? Are you hungry?"

"Oh, no, no," I said, all brisk business dialing my phone. My cousin, now grown, picked up the phone. "Can you come get me?" I asked my cousin when she picked up.

"I'm outside now," she said. She was driving my aunt's giant SUV and she was blond, tan, eighteen, and charming beyond belief. I heard her loud music playing in the background.

"She's here," I told Billy and packed up my stuff.

"I'll walk outside with you," Billy said. "Time for a smoke."

"My dad hated smoking so much."

Billy laughed and retrieved a pack of Winstons from his pocket. "I know."

My cousin was parked by the entrance. Outside, I turned to Billy, unsure of what to do. I held out my hand for him to shake and he pulled me toward him in an embrace.

I hugged him back tightly, thinking of the hug I never gave my dad. I thought about that hug all the time.

"Thank you," I said, opening the door to the SUV and sliding in.

My cousin clicked her cell phone shut and looked at Billy Temple. "Oh," she said. "He looks so nice." He stood outside, lighting his cigarette. He looked upward as he exhaled the smoke.

"One second," I said and jumped suddenly out of the car, walking back toward Billy. "I don't really smoke," I said, "but could I have one of those?"

Billy smiled and took a cigarette from his pack, handing it to me. "But right about now you could use one, right?" He pulled me back in quick, kissed me on the top of the head, and then turned away. It seemed impossible to move from the spot, but I got back in the car, dazed, holding my unlit cigarette.

"We can go now," I said.

I looked at my reflection in the passenger-side mirror. As a child I'd had long wavy hair and my dad brushed it a hundred stokes at a time. Sometimes I cried and he would tell me, "It hurts to be beautiful."

———————

AT BILLY'S FUNERAL, I'm astounded by how stunning the summer day is—so different from my father's frigid December Mass and January burial—and by how much the ache of my dad's absence still thumps around inside my body. I want to be a better person than this. I want not to enjoy the sensation of the sun on my bare arms and not to think about my own father when someone else's had died so recently, but I can't help it.

———•———

AT MY PARENTS' wedding in 1977, my dad wore a white ruffled tuxedo shirt with no tie, collar unfastened to show off a Tom Selleck-esque tuft of chest hair. My mom's gown was ivory with long lace sleeves. She wore a fingertip-length cap veil over her short haircut and two delicate strands of pearls around her neck. They stood beneath a huppah to say their vows and when my dad smashed the ceremonial glass with his foot everyone yelled out, "Mazel tov!"

The breaking of the glass, despite the cheers and mazel tov'ing that accompanies it, is actually, as I, a Jew by birthright alone, understand it, meant to be a solemn event. It signifies the destruction of the Holy Temple in Jerusalem more than two thousand years ago. It's about tempering the joy of the occasion with a reminder about the fragility of life and love.

———•———

I MET MY husband, Nick, in 2010 at a Vietnamese restaurant in Brooklyn. We were introduced by mutual friends and by coincidence he was from Rhode Island, as well. We played the familiar game—what high school, whose cousin—and within minutes we knew countless people in common. I was going through a bad spell, still smarting from a breakup that was now over a year old; I was working in a windowless office and drinking too much. When the group of us, including my future husband, sat down to order our meals, I requested a round of tequila shots for the table, which seemed to confuse most of the people there.

A few weeks later, I was with a friend and we ran into Nick at a bar. He was as drunk as almost anyone I'd ever seen and trying, without much success, to eat an empanada. He stroked my friend's long, wavy hair and got her phone number. When they broke up, Nick and I fell in love. It was, in its way, the story of every romance.

We were dating four months when I helped Nick check himself into alcohol detox and then watched with amazement as he got and stayed sober. I curbed my drinking as well. There was no more coming home from work to slowly work my way through a bottle of wine. Now I came home, picked up my dog, and walked over to Nick's apartment where we ate a ridiculous amount of sweets and both of us got better and better.

Once, while we were visiting family in Rhode Island, I asked Nick if we could visit my mother's grave. It was something I hadn't done in years, though I'd spent so much time researching her death.

I explained to Nick that at a Jewish cemetery we left a rock, not flowers. Just a token to show we'd been there. That we'd been thinking of them. Looking at the inscription on her grave, JOAN CARROLL 1954–1984, WIFE, MOTHER,

DAUGHTER, SISTER, FRIEND, I suddenly realized how much had been taken from her. I was thirty-two at the time—I'd outlived her already by two years and still felt like I'd not done a quarter of what I hoped to do with my life.

I'd been researching her, I'd been wondering about her, I'd been imagining who she would have been if she lived. But I never really thought about who she was as a person, as a woman who existed entirely outside of my existence. In some ways, I'd become complicit in her disappearance. I'd allowed her to become a specter: the doomed mother. I'd painted a portrait of her out of cigarette smoke and newspaper clippings. I'd let her be defined by the men and sex and drugs that made up the final moments of her life. Standing there, I felt ashamed. She was Joan Goldman Carroll, who struggled, who was loved, whose life was stolen. She was a woman, in the world, fearless, hopeful, careless, everything we all are.

When it was time to leave, Nick had two rocks to leave at her grave. One from me and one from him. We were thinking about her. We remembered her. I promised her that.

NICK AND I were married in Newport, Rhode Island, in front of about one hundred people. His brother became an Internet minister to marry us. My sister stood next to him and read from Justice Kennedy's majority decision in *Obergefell v. Hodges* requiring all states to recognize same-sex marriage. Ann-Marie, who had been there for me since

I was six, sat along with her four brothers and her mother, my Grandma Ann. My Aunt Sandy cried and gripped me hard, told me how much she loved me and how proud of me she was. Reba and Alex, still so much in my life, gave a joint toast. In lieu of tossing my bouquet of yellow roses, I gave it to my grandmother, my sweet, sweet grandmother, now suffering from Alzheimer's, who accepted it with her hand clutching her heart. It rained, and everyone told us that was good luck. I felt like if I didn't keep dancing I would drop from exhaustion so I did, for hours, barely getting a chance to speak to anyone, sweaty and focused.

Afterward, in our hotel suite, I drew a hot bath in the luxurious soaking tub, unhooked my wedding dress, letting it fall to the floor, and climbed in. I dunked my head under the water and when I came up there were a dozen tiny fake lashes floating around me.

We had walked down the aisle to Beethoven's Ninth, fourth movement, which I've still not seen in person, and in addition to my bouquet I carried the Hebrew Bible my mother had carried down the aisle when she married my dad. My husband smashed the glass on the first try, to raucous applause.

Sometimes Nick will send me a link about a TV show, or new movie, or concert tour with a note about how it seems like something my dad would have liked. He understands him in a way that nobody who ever knew him alive possibly could. The fact that he cannot only understand but grow to really appreciate such a mercurial person from description alone makes me think two things—that I married the right man, and that my mom and dad live on in everything I am.

When I ask people about my parents, one of the things I look for is repetition. I've noticed that every person has essentially the same thing to say about my parents' marriage: "They just got each other." "They were soul mates, but they did their own thing and they met up at the end of the day." "They accepted each other but they did their own thing." "They just fit." And this too: My mom told my dad that I was all she needed, and if he wanted another baby, he could go to the baby store and buy one himself because it wasn't happening.

———◆———

THE DAY AFTER our wedding, my aunt tells me that my grandmother had refused to let go of the bouquet of roses I'd given to her. She had to be cajoled into letting them go so my aunt could put them in a vase. My grandmother doesn't remember who I am, exactly, but she understands something else, something more important. She doesn't remember what happened to my mom. But I do. I remember. I remember you, Mom. And Dad, you were not that bad a guy. I promise never to forget.

ACKNOWLEDGMENTS

This book would have been impossible to write without the support of my family. Thank you Ann-Marie Carroll Cutlip, Sandra Goldman, Hayley Rettenmyer, Ruth Goldman, Taylor Carroll, the Solingers, the Goldmans, the Aloisios, and the Catuccis.

I don't know what I've done to deserve such wonderful friends and I don't know what I would do without you. Thank you Rebecca Friedman, Alexandra Griffin, Colleen Lawrie, Lee Pinkas, Urcella Di Pietro, David Ramsey, Sean Bottai, Julie Cohen, Rachel Riederer, Mike Spies, Melissa Kirsch, Elizabeth Mann, and everyone else who puts up with me even though I'm chronically late, totally unreliable, and usually hungry.

Thank you to the people who helped me put the pieces of this story together especially Mark Morse, John MacAndrew, Audrey Shaw, Dan Limbaugh, Thomas Matlack, Ruth Ferrazano, and Dean Starkman.

I am so grateful to Helen Atsma for acquiring this book, and to Libby Burton for taking it on and editing it with grace, candor, wisdom, and patience that borders on magical. Thank you to my agent, David Patterson, for making this happen.

Thank you David Leavitt, Jill Ciment, Padgett Powell, Mary Robison, Stephen O'Connor, Richard Hoffman, Frederick Reiken, Kathy Robbins, Rachelle Bergstein, Roy and Stephanie Katzovicz, Greg Racz and Alexa Jervis, Daniel Jones, Ada Calhoun, Sara Millstein, the MacDowell Colony, and the New York Foundation for the Arts.

And finally, thank you Nick, for your unwavering support and guidance. Who would have thought that I'd marry a nice boy from Rhode Island? Thank you for making a space in our lives for Joan and Kevin. I love you.

ABOUT THE AUTHOR

LEAH CARROLL lives in Brooklyn, New York. She graduated from Emerson College, and received an MFA in fiction from the University of Florida. She is the recipient of fellowships from the New York Foundation for the Arts and the MacDowell Colony.